THE
GRAVE
IN MY
SOUL

*Abortion…Consequences,
Regrets, Lessons & Blessings*

Lisa A. DeRoché

This is a work of nonfiction.

Dedication

I dedicate this book to my parents who if not for them I may not have been born. Their encouragement about pursuing education is what inspired me to write a book and pursue a PhD. Their coaching methods were not always conventional, however I appreciate them for making me into the woman I am today.

The Grave in My Soul

Preface

This book is an autobiographical novel of sorts. It is the story of my life based on my own perspective and reality. Michelle Obama said, "You're story is what you have, it is all you will ever have. Everyone is carrying around an unseen history". She is right. I had these grandiose ideas and thoughts of how important and unique my life was when I was growing up. I now know that each of our lives is unique. I decided to tell the story about my own to the world.

I wrote in diaries since the 7th grade in order to help me make sense of all my experiences growing up which at times were very challenging and emotional. I captured almost everything in writing as a therapeutic exercise for myself to get through them. Often times, life was so complicated and difficult to interpret for me that I wrote everything down while I analyzed it all in my head. Writing the words down on paper helped me to decipher what I was feeling; since many times, I could not explain exactly how I felt in any given moment. Since I began writing at the young age of 12, I suppose I always hoped that one day, I would have a purposeful story to tell. I continued to write through adulthood and created this memoir as a guide to aide young people as they face their own challenges throughout life.

The Grave in My Soul begins with my parents losing three kids in a car accident on the island of Jamaica a few years before I was born. If not for this tragedy, they may not have tried again to have more children. Once my mother was pregnant with me, my father always told the story of wanting a little girl because he knew a girl would take care of him after already having several children, many of them boys. At the time I was born, the doctor came out and joked around with him.

"Mr. Crawford, you have a boy!"

"No doc, you have it wrong, you must have it wrong."

The doctor said, "Yes, Mr. Crawford you're right, it's a girl, Congratulations!"

My father really wanted a little girl and he would have that one last girl upon migrating to New York from Jamaica. Born in Brooklyn and raised on Long Island, New York, I made poor choices with unprotected sex which resulted in me having two abortions, the first of which was during high school. The second one while living a freedom filled lifestyle in college. My story includes being raised by a very strict Jamaican father, maneuvering through an intense relationship with a man who eventually became the father of my first daughter and eventually reconnecting and marrying my first love from junior high school. We raised a blended family of five children together; and throughout it all I maintained a praying heart.

Ultimately, I wrote this book because I want people, especially young people, to use it as a reminder to be more thoughtful when making decisions than I was. I want to mentor young people and remind them to stop and consider the consequences of a decision prior to making them which they may not realize are poor at the time or the lasting affects these decisions may have. I also want to showcase that no one is perfect and you can make mistakes in life and recover from them well as long as you have a plan.

I used the subject matter of abortion as a real example since many suffer from having had the experience and have difficulty getting past the emotions of guilt and loss that come with this difficult choice. I could not get away from it. It was an experience that I went through and live with everyday. Not only was the loss from abortion a lingering experience for me, death in general has also been something that comes across my mind on a regular basis. I think about the concept of death as being so final yet we all must go through it, as apart of life yet it is often displayed as a very grave and negative concept. Although loss is final, it does not have to be discouraging and connected to so many terrible thoughts. We should talk more about loss, express our feelings of fear and worry related to loss and be comforted in knowing that we all live and must go through it. The cover of the book is not meant to be dark and scary. It is to show how heavy the conversation of abortion and loss can be no matter what perspective you have on it politically. More importantly, the book and its cover reflect that difficult things will happen however the important part is coming back from the experience. It is okay if the experience stays in your heart and soul as long as it doesn't hold you back from your blessings. It is important not to let the grave hold your body down but for your soul to live everlasting. That is the main message being expressed here.

This book took me several years to write, ten years to be exact. Writing is a difficult task, especially since some of the content brought up some traumatic memories for me that many might want to forget. However, writing was also calming to my soul. Based on following along the timeline of my diaries, I could recall the specific dates and actual events that I otherwise may not have remembered. Although I started this project in 2009, I didn't write at all for several of the intervening years. So many things got in the way of completing the book including work, school, life, the lack of motivation, and fear; the fear of being judged for my past. I was also fearful of being vulnerable and telling the truth about these things I had done that I wasn't very proud of. Instead I swallowed my fear and pride and forged forward with the hopes of being able to give back to someone else who is going through something. They may need to know they are not alone and that they can talk about it without fear. Why should we fear our past? It's the past and it's not coming back.

What I learned over the years is that even through mistakes, if you are passionate about something that makes you a better person, you will not let anything get in the way of getting it done. When you want to achieve great things, like getting a degree, interviewing for a better job, becoming an entrepreneur, you do what it takes to go after it. I also learned through my faith in God and my personal growth that I am proud of whom I am and of the woman I have become.

I was working on my PhD at the same time when I was most serious and consistent about writing. I started the Business Management program on my birthday on October 10th in 2016. You will come to find out throughout the book that many important events have happened on my birthday (1010). Although the major functional area of my program is business, my specialty is Human Resources, which has grown to be my passion. I had a quarterly school schedule with class in session for ten weeks followed by three week breaks in between quarters. This lasted for three years, including summers, for the coursework portion of the program. I attempted to write during school breaks. Often times, this was not easy because most of the time I wanted to relax after completing ten weeks of intensive research and coursework. However, I kept at it, kept setting short-term goals and moving through them. I have passed my comprehensive exams, on the second try and now which makes me a PhD candidate. The last phase is writing the dissertation and I am giving myself one year to complete it.

I found out later in life that it is important to give yourself credit for your successes and to celebrate the small wins you accomplish to keep yourself motivated. I learned that best while working on my coursework which was an online program and at times a very lonely process. Once I changed my perspective and looked at the required discussion posts, assignments, and papers that I struggled to get done as a potential accomplishment itself, I realized there is truly nothing to fear but fear itself. Each time I completed a task, I celebrated by taking some time to do something for myself that I enjoyed like going out to eat or visiting with friends.

My writing history has shown how I have grown over the years, how my writing has improved from diary to diary and how much stronger I became over time. What I know that has not changed over the years is my love for God. Through it all, I continued to ask God for strength to get through every task, every rough family interaction, every career decision and every waking moment. My love for God has always been my strength.

This is the story of my life that was intended and set up for me since the day I was born on October, 10, 1969. I really hope you enjoy the book; it is an outpouring of my heart and life to you all from only my perspective. If you have a different perspective, consider writing the sequel ☺. Note all of the names have been changed to protect the innocent.

Buried deep in your spirit lays your truths;
this is the Grave in My Soul.

Acknowledgements

I want to take this time to acknowledge some very important people in my life starting with who inspired me to stay on track: My parents; Pansy Muir Hume and Fitzbert Crawford. If it wasn't for them making the decision to keep me I would not have made it into this world to live and tell this story. Their example of hard work and perseverance held me to a high standard to ensure great performance in my life even though they were not equipped to school me on the American way of life and what to expect in handling corporate environments and other difficult experiences. They taught me faith, education and family values. They did their best with what they had and I am extremely grateful.

I want to give a special shout out to my first love, Larry. I knew that I was going to be with Larry for the rest of my life when we first met in the 7th grade. He was my first love and will be my last love. Thank you babe; I appreciate all of your support on this very important project. It was he who told me to make it happen when I decided I was ready to talk about my experiences with abortion publicly. I was really apprehensive about doing it and he supported me all the way. Thank you for crying together with me through all the hard times and believing in me the entire time.

I want to thank my children Javona, Jazmin and Gabriel and my bonus children Britney and Brandon. Thanks to them, I have a beautiful story to tell about my amazing growth as a Mom and bonus Mom and I can watch their growth as wonderful human beings living in this life.

I want to thank all of my sisters and brothers (too many to name here) for being a part of me and with me at various times in my life. I also want to thank my extended family, my mother-in-law, Gloria, three sisters in law; two of whom passed away while writing this book and my many cousins, nieces, nephews and grand nieces and nephews. I would also like to thank my ex-almost mother-in-law Grandma Shirley who never gave up on me while raising all of my children. She cared about all of us as if we were her own and because of that I am very grateful. I also want to thank all of my friends that I have made since grade school through, college and in my work life, all of you. You all know who you are. I also want to thank Auntie Jean for praying with me at a time when I needed it the most. You gave me the inspiration, motivation and hope I needed to get past my long standing feelings of guilt.

I finally want to thank and send a special shout out to my grandson Josiah aka Jojo who is literally my twin. I never thought I could have so much love for someone other than my own kids that I do for my grandson. He won't be reading this book anytime soon, but when he does maybe he will remember the moment in my car in the summer of 2018 when he was returning from visiting his Grampy in the Bronx and he asked me why I never go there with him. I explained to him that Grampy is his mother's father and my ex-boyfriend and we are no longer together and haven't been for more than 25 years. His response in his own words at 9 years old was "mind blown!" After reading my book when he is a little older, he will have a better understanding of the ups and downs of relationships. He can also share the story with my other 2 grandchildren; his cousins Lyla and Ava (baby bump now coming soon).

The Grave in My Soul

Table of Contents

The Grave in My Soul

CONSEQUENCES

1

My First Love

I moved to Long Island in the first grade from Queens. Though I was born in East New York, Brooklyn in Wycoff Heights Hospital, we lived in those boroughs for a very short time. While growing up on Myron Street on Long Island in New York, some might say that I was a real nerd. I was very much into reading and writing and I loved to play instruments like flute and piano. I also wore glasses in the 1st grade. Myron Street was a tree-lined, suburban street with beautiful houses and lots of color. Our house was the biggest house on the block. I lived there with my parents, three brothers and one sister. I was a daughter to Jamaican parents who had me in 1969, three years after losing three kids and three other family members in a fatal car accident in Jamaica. They were in the process of migrating to the United States to find a better life for them and their other children, many of whom were left behind in Jamaica. The accident deterred their arrival for a short time before they officially moved to their first house in Brooklyn.

It was a beautiful, warm January day in 1966 when my parents were dropped off at the Norman Manley airport in Kingston, Jamaica, excited about boarding a flight on their journey to New York. They were driven to the airport by a van driver who was a friend of my father's. The 7-passenger van was filled with several of mom and Dad's family members including two of Daddy's kids from another mother, Joy and Donovan, along with my mother and Dad's son Junior (aka Barrington). My Uncle Alva, my mother's brother, was in the van along with my Aunt Lola's brother and a cousin who was visiting from college. They made a pit stop to say goodbye to my Aunt Monica, my mom's sister, since she didn't live too far from the airport. Uncle Alva decided to stay there and not follow along to the airport.

Lucky for him, because on the return ride from the airport a large truck cut off the van going around a steep curve; it side swiped the van which turned over repeatedly and literally snapped in half. If you know anything about the roads in Jamaica, especially at that time, they were very fragile, hilly, unpaved and close together. Most roads were one-way and very dangerous. A total of six people died in the van that day. My Mom and Dad buried three kids after that accident, including my brother Junior (Barrington) who was only five years old at the time. I imagine this was a devastating loss for my parents. At that time I had four other siblings (that I knew of). I don't think my Mom and Dad had planned on having any more kids at their ages of

31 and 40, but after losing three children in the accident they were compelled to try again and this is how the story of my life begins…

In 1975 we settled on Long Island in Nassau County which is the southern part of Long Island. As a first grader, I went to Cornelius Court School which housed Kindergarten and 1st grade students only. I remember walking home from school which was a short walk down the block and around the corner from my house on Myron Street. Nowadays, kids can't walk anywhere alone at that age.

Once I moved up into 2nd grade at the California Ave. elementary school I began playing the flute and loved every minute of it. I used to often spend time sitting out in my backyard playing the flute. My select music class was preparing to record an album that would be sold nationwide. I played the flute in the ensemble band I was involved in a ton of activities related to music, took piano lessons and participated in youth chorus at church. My three brothers who also lived with me played guitar and drums. We were heavily involved at the United Methodist Church of Hempstead and quickly assimilated into our very segregated community. We were the only black people on the block, but it was evident that people really liked us since I was able to make several white friends on the block very quickly who I played with all the time. We would play jax, hop scotch, tag, hide-n-seek and Ringolevio 1-2-3, 1-2-3, 1-2-3. In Ringolevio there are two teams, each with the same number of players. There are no time limits and no intermissions. Each team has two jails, typically it was someone's front stoop. One team counts while the other team goes to hide. Team two goes after members of team one and subsequently brings them back to the jail one by one until they are all caught. Once you grab someone you chant "Ringolevio, 1-2-3, 1-2-3, 1-2-3. If the person breaks free before the chant is finished they can run. If caught and sent to jail, someone on the hiding team must tag the jail to set those caught free until the whole team is caught. This game could go on for hours.

My Dad was a hard-working construction man, a member of the Local 14-14b union for operating engineers. He did this work his for many years until he retired. He was a short, stocky man with medium brown skin and not much hair, just a short, frail afro. He had big rough hands from working in the construction business. He operated huge cranes that move materials at work sites. He did this work in Jamaica and carried this trade and his expertise with him over to America. My Dad had a rough exterior; a deep voice and an empowering approach even though he was not that tall. He was very strict with me and my siblings, but on the inside he was my loving, jovial, kind-hearted father. Daddy worked from 7am - 3pm and left very early in the morning for work.

My mom worked in the Central Supply department of Franklin Hospital in Valley Stream which is now Northwell Valley Stream. My mom is a beautiful woman with a medium build and at the time had very long, dark wavy hair. She looked like an Indian, possibly

Cherokee, as did her brothers and sisters. Back in the day they called her "coolie" for her appearance. The term was originally used to describe indentured laborers from Asia who migrated to Guyana, Trinidad & Tobago and Jamaica. However, in her case, it also reflected a particular look of someone who was mixed with Indian heritage. My mom worked the 3 -11pm shift so that someone was always home with us as young kids.

For several years after moving to Long Island, all my friends on the block were white and I didn't necessarily know the difference until 6th grade when two other black girls my age moved into the neighborhood from Queens. They used to make fun of how I talked. I used to say to them"come on (you guys), let's go to the park" or "hey (you guys), let's go to the store" and they would say to me, "don't say (you guys)" because according to them I sounded so white, they'd tell me"say ya'll!" I never thought there was a difference in my diction from theirs but my wording was different. Today, as a black person if called out as someone who "speaks so well" by a white person, it can be considered offensive; as if not good enough to speak the Queen's English. In other words, speaking standard, pure or correct might be seen as unusual for a black girl vs speaking slang. Coming from their perspective right out of Queens to Long Island, the culture had shifted; the streets and neighbors would be different. The way I talked was normal to me, but when the girls pointed out the difference in how I said certain words I never wondered what the basis of the difference was until much later on. I recognized that growing up in a mostly white neighborhood on Long Island did give you a different perspective.

I really enjoyed reading. I often read out loud when I was by myself. My parents filled the house with Encyclopedia's when I was growing up so I often took them down from the bookshelf in our den and read them. Encyclopedia sales people were common back in those days. They came to your house and sold you an entire stack of Britannicas, or you could get them in sets of four. The books were sorted by alphabet from A-Z. I am sure I have looked through every set. If not just for fun, I would use them as a reference for a report I was writing in school. See, back then we didn't have Google or the Internet like we have today so we had to literally find information in books and other resources. Shortly after the girls kidded me about my verbal communication style, these two girls from Queens became family to me.

Tracey and Sam were sisters. They were tall, slim and brown-skinned, one a little lighter than the other, and their background was Jamaican like me. This was so meaningful to me and my family. We all spoke the same language and came from the same place, and there was a fast connection with them right away. We would later find out that we had some family members in common so immediately began calling each other cousins.

The girls had an older brother named Rob who used to hang out with my two brothers, Tony and Will. When Rob was four he lost one eye when he was struck with a sling shot by another little boy who used a nail as his chosen weapon. It catapulted into Rob's face while they were outside playing. From that point on he only saw life through one eye. His vantage point was very different from the rest of us, but that never slowed down his genius. He was always building some crazy new invention.

All of us spent many days and nights hanging out in our neighborhood on Manor Pkwy where Tracey, Sam and Rob lived. A few years into our friendship, my brother Will was working on a moped in Rob's garage with a bunch of other guys. That night, my parents, my brothers and I had just come from a family party in Queens and it was pretty late. Will asked my Dad if he could go around the corner to Rob's house and my Dad specifically told Will not to go out that night because it was already late when we returned from the party. But he left anyway. Will had a tendency to want to do his own thing and not follow the rules of the house. He was out in the garage with Rob and the other guys working on fixing a moped. Mopeds were a favorite mode of transportation around that time for young guys on Long Island if you could afford to have one. The moped was turned upside down and they were operating on it like surgeons. The chain link and the motor was revving as loud as a Mustang car engine. While tinkering and hammering away on the chain with some tools, out of nowhere a large lug nut spun out of the chain, rotating rapidly. It fired off of the chain like a gunshot directed right at my brother Will and hit him square in his left eye. He grabbed his face and screamed in horror. There was blood everywhere.

Will was immediately rushed to the hospital at Nassau County Medical Center. My parents were called on one of those late night phone calls no one wants to get indicating there was an accident. He was taken into surgery and shortly after the surgeon advised my parents that he lost his sight in that eye and right there his life was changed in an instant. He was in the hospital for a few weeks. We were all devastated. Now Rob & Will had something in common.

The days of hanging out on Manor Pkwy were times I will never forget, the good times and the bad times came like the wind. Tracey and Sam's house was one of the few places that I could go without my Dad being worried about me; or so he thought. It was during this time I met my first love.

Tracey and a guy named Spencer were fast friends in Turtle Hook Junior High School. They had a few classes together. Spencer was light-skinned, tall and very handsome in my eyes. He had really dark features beyond his light complexion which I would describe as beige, like the color of pralines and cream ice cream. His hair was dark black with a short afro and his eyebrows were really black, thick and bushy. He was bow-legged and everything about him made me nervous. When we met, Tracey was in 8th grade, Spencer was in 9th grade, and I was in 7th grade.

I ran into Spencer all the time in the hallways and then in the neighborhood since he spent a lot of time on Manor Pkwy and lived around the corner from us. For whatever reason, when Spencer and I met for the first time, we clicked immediately and became junior high school sweethearts instantly. It truly felt like love at first sight. He and I lived literally a hop of a fence and one block away from each other so it was a regular thing for us to be hanging out in our neighborhood together, smoking a joint or just laughing and trying to be cool on the streets.

Tracey's house was located right on the corner at Manor Pkwy and this was the hang out for all us local kids. Their parents were very cool especially, their Mom, who I called Aunt Joy. She was a short, sexy woman with a lot of hips and body to back it up. She had fashion sense for days and always wore exotic outfits with wraps and ethnic earrings in her ears. She didn't wear much makeup. She had more of a natural beauty and air to her persona which was very attractive and powerful. Their Dad was unusually tall and had really long dreadlocks and his mere presence in a room used to scare everyone. He appeared to be the image of the pictures of Black Jesus with a beard, long wooly hair and eyes of fire. When he came around, his scent filled the room like the effervescent sweet smells of ganja were flowing through his body and trailing behind his shadow. His height filled up the doorway like a big shadow from a cartoon scene and when he entered the room he would appear slowly and dramatically like the scene of a scary movie and leave without us even knowing it. All of us kids called him "The Big Dread". We spent many days and nights in the basement on Manor Pkwy playing video games and watching ourselves on video camera. Rob the local genius set up his video camera in the basement so that we could all watch ourselves act silly on camera. There was no sound, so you couldn't hear what we were saying, thank God, but you could play back all the activities and watch our antics as we performed various musical routines with lyrics and dance moves included. Half the time we sat around drinking, smoking cigarettes and weed or watching our mouth moving on the video playback. You could hear the music but never hear what we were saying. We used to listen to the radio station WBAU that operated out of the local college at the time. The D.J. was Dr. Dre from Long Island. He was not the West Coast producer and gangster rapper. He was a D.J. for the Beastie Boys and co-host of "Yo! MTV Raps". Dr. Dre and his best friend Ed Lover also starred in a movie called "Who's the Man?" in 1993, however before all of that he used to be a radio D.J. at Adelphi University. We were always bumping with him and listening from the basement on Manor Pkwy. I considered the basement on Manor Pkwy my second home, and where I found security.

Going back to around the end of 6th grade I noticed that my mom and Dad were fighting a lot. My mom was always asking my

Dad to go places that he never wanted to go. He was a couch potato for many years. He'd lay in his lazy boy chair day and night and just ask for his food and drinks to be delivered to him until he found the energy to get out of the chair and head up to his bedroom which was about the same time every night, 9 pm. Earlier on that year, my mom made a decision to take a trip to London to visit her brother, Carlton. She went alone, apparently because Daddy did not want to go even after she arranged for his ticket and everything. Shortly after she got back from the trip, the fighting continued. My Dad left for work really early in the morning and there were some days, I would be on my way to school and my mom would be on the phone on a long distance call with someone she would say was "her friend". One time I spoke to "her friend" because she wanted me to talk to him. His name was JC. I didn't quite understand it at the time, but not long after this, my mom told me that she and my Dad were getting a divorce.

After she made a decision to divorce my Dad, she left the house with almost nothing since I really don't think my Dad wanted it to happen at all. He was hopelessly in love with her. You could tell by the way he looked at her and in a way, maybe he saw her as a trophy for all his hard work. In his mind, he won this beautiful woman to come home to and raise all his children, but for my mother, I am sure it was not that gratifying at all.

At that time she asked me if I wanted to leave with her, but I didn't think I should go. I didn't want to leave my new junior high school, my friends, my big house and my room to travel around with her going God knows where since she didn't have a house or a place to stay. I also didn't want to leave my Dad alone, wondering how he would manage without her. I felt somewhat torn, but in the same vein, I didn't feel like I had a choice but to stay. I felt fine where I was. Little did I know at the time that my father had made it clear to her that she was not going to take me with her. From there on in, I put all my energy into my first love.

Spencer and I started to get closer, and every chance I had to break away and spend time with him, I did. Back in 1981, all we were doing was kissing and touching each other, learning each other's parts. I wore Spencer's name belt to school every chance I could because at that time, name belts were some sort of badge of honor...this told everyone, I AM HIS GIRL. If you were wearing someone's name belt, it was proof that you were in a serious relationship.

I used to pass Spencer's classes and peek in on him, and when my friends and I saw him in the hallway we'd laugh and giggle and say, "There he go, there he go." My heart used to pound incessantly and flutter anytime he was around. Now I know where the term butterflies in your stomach came from. After about a year passed, we got closer. He used to write me beautiful love letters and ended the letters with Lisa and Spencer in a heart dated 11-1-82, which was the date we truly hooked up. When I say hooked up, I mean when we first started having sex. By then I was 14 and in the 8th grade.

We spent an entire first year just getting to know each other, laughing a lot, talking, spending time together up late on the phone; all the things you do when you are falling in love. I braided his hair and, at that time, it was long enough to do plaits. I loved this feeling of new friendship and closeness with him. Of course, since he was three years older than me, a lot of the time Spencer and I were together he wanted it to go further. I felt so scared and just not ready to do anything more than just fool around. I kept putting him off, giving him excuses, pretty much any excuse I could think of. At one point he told me that if I didn't have sex with him he would have to start seeing other girls just for sex. As a young girl with no experience, I didn't know this was a manipulative statement. I took it to heart and told him okay, that was fine and he should go out there and go be with other girls (and have sex) because I certainly was not ready to have sex and I didn't want him to keep pressuring me and getting frustrated that I wouldn't do it with him.

Not long after that he did start to mention other girls (older girls) that he was going to see or talk to and I acted like I did not care when it was really burning me up inside. I was hurt and felt betrayed and worthless. I felt that it was unfair to have to compete with other girls for his affection. If he liked me or even loved me, why wouldn't he just wait until I was ready to commit to a sexual relationship?

At this point I felt my value was limited because I would not take the relationship to the next level and engage in sexual intimacy like a full-grown women. This feeling and game playing went on for about three months, until finally I couldn't stand it anymore. One day I called Spencer up out of the blue and told him I was ready and that he should meet me at my house the next morning when I knew no one would be home.

2

Losing My Virginity

That day I cut school and so did Spencer. After everyone left the house that morning I anticipated him coming to the door every five minutes while a ball of nerves grew in my stomach. I wasn't sure if he would knock or ring the bell. When the doorbell rang I proceeded down the steps of my high ranch home and welcomed him into my house. At this point my nerves were on overdrive for a few reasons. I wondered if someone would see him come to the door and know that I had cut school and was at home planning to have my first intimate encounter. I was scared that someone would tell my Dad that I had a boy in the house with no one home and that might get me killed. I also wondered if I was truly ready to be in the most vulnerable position of my life. Once I let him in, I looked outside the door and down the block both ways to make sure no one else was on the block when he walked through the door.

When Spencer arrived he greeted me hello with a hug and a brief kiss and we went straight up to my bedroom on the same path I came down a minute ago to meet him at the door. Each step felt like I had iron weights attached to my feet. I wasn't sure I should be going up the steps again. I wasn't sure that I was making the right decision. I almost hesitated and changed my mind. I was so nervous I thought I was going to get sick. He followed me up the steps and I wondered if he was looking at my butt as I walked up the steps ahead of him. I am pretty sure he was.

We went into my bedroom which was the second door on the right of the landing past the pink and green bathroom, past the huge floor to ceiling mirror staring at me, and past the locked door to my father's room. We sat on the bed and talked for a few minutes. I really didn't know what to do first, but without delay or hesitation, we lay down on my bed and he immediately took out the items in his pocket, his keys, his money, and a condom. He started to get undressed by taking off his pants followed by his t-shirt. I took his lead and took off my pants and my shirt and sat down on the bed. He came over and sat down next to me. He pulled me close and started to kiss me and then he quickly reached inside my bra to caress my breasts. I put my hands inside his underwear and could feel that his penis was growing. It was getting harder and bigger by the moment. He moved to the side of the bed and picked up the condom from the table and started to rip it open and take it out of the package. I asked him how is it supposed to go on and he opened it up and showed me how to put it on. We started kissing some more and after I started to relax a little, he moved his hands down towards my panties and put his fingers inside me. He started with one finger, then two and then added one more as he saw that I was beginning to lower my guard and loosen my tense back. At that point he started to get very erect and moved me into a position where he could pull my legs open. Then he got up on his knees, pulled my panties down to my ankles and made an attempt to put his penis inside of me. It didn't go in at first, I guess because I was a virgin and not really that wet or that turned on. He fingered me a little more until it felt ready and then he tried putting his penis inside me again. This time he pushed it in a little harder and I squirmed a bit and made a whining sound as the pain or pressure I was feeling was somewhat unusual to me. At that point his penis went inside my body and he began to move his body in and out and up and down and in and out on top of mine until I assumed he felt himself ejaculating. I assumed that's what was happening since I could see him panting and breathing faster and faster. Then his breathing slowed down to a normal pace and he moved over from on top of me to lay down and there he stared at the ceiling for about 30 seconds. Eventually he looked at me and said, "Thank you babe," and then pulled me close and kissed me. I was still in shock and feeling overwhelmed by what had just taken place. My body was still in the room, but my brain had temporarily stepped out of the room and was trying to determine what my body was going through.

At that point I was in so much pain I started whimpering and crying, wondering why this did not feel as good to me as it looked like it felt to him! After I got over the pain and shock I immediately became ecstatic to know that I'd had sex for the first time with who I felt was the love of my life. I thought that now maybe he'd love me forever also and I'd never have to worry about him wanting to have sex ever again with other girls. Well, boy was I wrong, because that is just not how it works. If only I knew at that time to be true to myself and not feel like I had to give up my body to be loved by someone else. Over time, I learned that the hard way. He left immediately following the encounter because we were both pretty nervous about him being caught in my house. I stayed home for the rest of the day and ended up telling my father that I was home sick that day.

Now that I had been through my first time and I was over the initial shock of it all, Spencer and I started to have sex more frequently. We did it at my house, in my room, behind the garage where it was very much hidden and no one would know. We did it at his house, in his bed where Spencer lived with his mom, stepfather and three sisters. We even had sex in his mom's bed one time. This experience of not just having sex, but having sex in a parent's bedroom, made me feel like I was special and grown up too. I started to enjoy sex more and did not feel the pain I'd felt initially. The way he treated me made me feel like I was the best thing that ever happened to him.

Spencer continued to ask me to braid his hair and do the silly things we always did. At one point it was growing out and it was fun to put tiny little twists in it. We were having a really fun and youthful time enjoying each other's company and acting like we were a married couple. I had a vision that one day this fantasy would come true. I told my two best friends what I had done, but I never gave them any of the details. They were shocked and surprised that I had gone all the way with Spencer. They wanted all the details, but I kept it simple and brief.

At one point my friends used to seem jealous and say I was spending too much time with him. They said he didn't really love me. During this time Aunt Joy had a talk with me and told me I was not presenting myself as a young lady because I was seen kissing Spencer on the street and it just wasn't a good look. She said it was embarrassing and not lady like. I figured everyone was jealous and didn't support me and I just did not want to hear it. I couldn't understand why there wasn't any support from my friends on my new found love. I couldn't understand why they weren't as happy about this as I was.

Not long after these love months passed, my Dad got wind of how much time I was spending with Spencer and he began arguing with me all the time to leave him alone because he thought I was too young. He wanted me to end the "friendship". God forbid I call it a relationship. I didn't want to listen, but at that time I was so very afraid of my father that I didn't have a choice but to listen to him. I was also a Daddy's girl since my mom was no longer around. At times I felt more like his wife. I was more often than not confined to the house and was not allowed to go out to many places. I spent many days and nights washing and ironing his clothes, and cooking for him and my three brothers. My sister had moved out long before. I felt like I was living in a nightmare all alone. I yearned for the love and attention I was receiving from Spencer, but my father and others were doing everything they could to block it from me.

So one night I met Spencer on the corner of his block of Walton Ave. and I told him the situation. I told him my Dad was very upset with how much time we were spending together and that he was no longer accepting of me spending so much time with a "man" friend, so right there I broke it off. I was devastated, and so was he. At least I wanted to believe that he was hurt like me. He comforted me and told me we would always be "special friends". I went home and cried my eyes out for the rest of the night. I tried to get on with my life the best way I could, but it wasn't always easy.

After the break-up with Spencer I never really allowed myself to get over him. Although he had girlfriends publicly, we still continued to have sex. I considered us what they call "secret lovers". No one knew it, but whatever chance we got we'd find hideout places and have sex. It reminds me of a song popular then, "Here we are, just the two of us together, takin' this crazy chance to be all alone. We both know that we should not be together, 'Cause if we're found out, it could mess up, both our happy homes. (He sings) I hate to think about us all meetin' up together, 'Cause as soon as I look at you it will show on my face, yeah, then they'll know that we've been loving each other. We can't let 'em know, no, no, no, We can't leave a trace. (BOTH of us sing) Secret Lovers, that's what we are, we shouldn't be together, but we can't let go, cuz what we feel is oh so real"!

There was a time that he was seeing two girls at the same time and I knew about it and I used to think wow they are both so dumb. How did they not know he was screwing around with both of them, or did they? There were many entries in my diary of my rants and raves about loving Spencer and hating Spencer for what I felt like was a cat and mouse game he was playing, not just with them, but with me too. I guess I was just as dumb as the others to be a part of this escapade, but I also knew that my father was not accepting of my relationship, so in many ways I was honoring his request publicly to not see Spencer.

There was one night in particular that Spencer and I shared together on New Year's Eve that I won't forget. I labeled it in my diary as "the most bugged night of my life!" The girls and I went to Times Square on New Year's Eve in 1984. We took the Long Island Railroad to watch the ball drop. We met Spencer and a group of other friends from my neighborhood there. We did a lot of walking that night in the city. One guy took us up into Harlem. They were buying cocaine and all kinds of other illegal drugs. At every street we stopped at we were actively clowning around and partaking in the drugs that were purchased. Some of us smoked weed and others were sniffing cocaine. We watched the ball drop in the middle of Times Square which is a huge tradition for New York. We felt excited to be a part of it.

After the ball dropped and we finished running the streets of the city we were back on the Long Island Railroad running in and out of the train cars, playing around. A couple of the guys were stealing gold chains from people and just acting up on the train. Spencer was giving me googlie eyes the whole night and I was totally feeling him and excited to be in his presence that night. He was acting sweet, talking to me in a sexy tone, and from time to time checking to see that I was okay. At one point on the train Spencer and one of the guys got into a huge brawl with some other wild kids on the train who we didn't know. Two of our friends ended up getting stabbed. One of the guys found the kids who did it, reported them to the conductor, and they ended up getting arrested and sent to jail. Once we got off the train we went straight to Hempstead General Hospital so the guys could get checked out. I was crying incessantly at one point because I thought Spencer was hurt, but my baby was alright. Going into that New Year I remember making New Year's resolutions, which I always do. That year's resolutions included promises to get good grades in school, to stay cool around everyone, to try to stop smoking cigarettes and to mind my own business. I found myself competing a lot in high school for attention and I was hoping to limit that need and just stay in my own corner.

When 1985 came it was Spencer's senior year in high school. At this time I was the most confused I'd ever been about my feelings for him. Some days I spent a lot of time on Manor Pkwy. at Tracey and Sam's and he would be around also. On this particular day in January, Spencer had come to their house with two of his friends. His actions towards me were at times confusing. I could never tell or wasn't sure whether he liked me or one of his other girls in that moment. One of the girls at the time was named Angela. She was a beautiful girl. She was half black and half Hispanic. She had long curly hair that she sometimes wore straightened. When she walked, she swayed like a dancer. She dressed like an exotic dancer with short mini skirts and flashy tops, had a great shape and an attitude full of fire. If it was Angela he really liked, I always wished he would stop fucking with me because it was very confusing, irritating and hurtful. At times he made eyes at me, want a kiss, want to have sex and I was so confused that I would just fall for it every time. Then he would just ignore me or act like I was not even there when Angela was around.

On the other hand, when Leslie was around, she got all of the attention. Leslie was a shorter, stocky light-skinned girl with short hair. She had a bit of an accent as if from the mid-west. She traveled a lot because her father was in the military and eventually ended up in the next town over from our hood. She hung around all the guys and got to go places with them because she had a car and drove them everywhere. I personally think they may have been using her; at least that's what I hoped. I couldn't bear the thought that Spencer really liked her.

One of the most ironic days of my life was just a few weeks after Spencer's prom. After school I told my father I was going to the library and, instead, I went over to Tracey's. Tracey, Sam and I went to their Aunt's house to babysit and Angela happened to come over to Manor Pkwy that day also. Angela's father was good friends with the Big Dread so she ended up at their house from time to time. The Leslie "thing" with Spencer was the whole entire conversation. Apparently Leslie told Spencer's mother and his family that he had quit his part-time job. Unfortunately, two of his sisters were having difficulty walking and eventually it got so bad over time that they couldn't walk at all. Since he was partially responsible for supporting his family financially with his two sisters unable to walk, his Mom and sisters had a fit about him quitting his job since he was still leaving home and telling them he was going to work. Spencer was furious with Leslie for telling his family his business. He was not happy at all about it and wanted to beat her ass.

Later on, Spencer and few of his friends came over to Manor Pkwy. We concocted a plan to beat Leslie's ass and I was at the center of the plan. We gathered at Leslie's bus stop near her house with a posse of people around 10 deep. We stood outside the bus stop which was in front of her house for a minute, circling the bus stop and talking shit to each other about kicking her ass, waiting for that bitch to get off the bus after school. When she did finally step outside the bus, Spencer approached her and asked her about what she told his mother about quitting his job. We surrounded her and waited for her to make the wrong move or say the wrong thing. She started to get loud with Spencer, yelling at him, and her mother came outside the house and was trying to quiet her down and get her inside.

I felt as if I had to take this opportunity to fight for Spencer's honor and show him that I had his back because I knew he wasn't going to hit her as much as he may have wanted to. I took that moment of opportunity and said fuck it and grabbed Leslie and slammed her on the ground. We started fighting at the bus stop. Sam jumped in on this and some dude pulled Sam off. In the heat of the moment Leslie's mother hit Sam. When I heard this, I started screaming and pounding on Leslie some more. When the fight was over I had all her hair in my hand! If I didn't love Spencer so much I wouldn't have done this. I was scared. I am not going to lie. Leslie screamed after us and called us all Spencer's "little friends". I was like, "Wait a minute bitch; I used to go out with him too, and longer than you, bitch!" I took that comment to mean that she wanted to appear as if she was older and more mature and more special to him than me. In my young mind, this was so important to me that he saw my loyalty for him, even though it was wrong to fight another girl over someone else's issue. Fighting was so barbaric and unnecessary.

During the summer of my 10th grade year Spencer was getting all geared up to go to his prom. I happened to see him and one of his best friends dressed up in all white Tuxedoes. Spencer had on the pink tie and his friend had on the baby blue tie. Of course, Spencer went to the prom with Angela who had doubled up in her class work to graduate in 1985 with Spencer rather than in 1986 when she was supposed to. I was so devastated to know they were going to the prom together. I always envisioned it would be me at the prom with him. I did all I could to not be upset about that evening. I cried my eyes out alone at home and I was as strong as I possibly could be in front of others. I eventually got over it.

By the time Spencer graduated and moved out of our high school I was going into the 11th grade. Now I needed to find my own way and maneuver new friendships with guys. Although there were a lot of guys that were interested in me, like guys in my class year and a few of the Five-Percent cats, I never really thought of anyone else seriously. In 1985 there was a group of guys who considered themselves members of the Five-Percent Nation, sometimes referred to as the Nation of Gods and Earths, or the Five Percent movement. This movement was started in Harlem in the 60s by former members of the Nation of Islam, specifically, Clarence 13x who became known as Allah the Father who was a former student of Malcolm X. These guys in high school who followed this movement came together to teach others that black people were the original people of the planet earth and therefore they were to be considered fathers or Gods and mothers or also called them Earths. Those who followed this movement were constantly talking about their Supreme Mathematics, a set of principles created by their father Allah. A lot of times you heard them in the hallway greeting each other saying, "Assalamaualaikum" which meant "Peace be unto you" and, "What's today's mathematics?" Then there would be a debate on that. I only believed in God, so I never found any of them or that talk interesting or real. In addition, I was still Spencer's side piece whenever he wanted it. The bad news is that all of the time I was still messing around with Spencer, I wasn't really protecting myself at all. He wasn't either. Of course, I got all the stories that "It doesn't feel the same with the condom", and "If you love me you will do it", etc. I did love him and at that point I would do anything he said so I listened and stopped using condoms with him when we had sex.

3

The Decision

By the time the summer of 1985 came I was enrolled in summer school. I didn't do that well that year and had to take social studies and science over again. I had Mr. Curry for Social studies, which I will never forget. Olivia, my best friend was in my summer school class. She has been my best friend since the 7th grade. We were also born a week apart so we so had many things in common and usually shared a birthday celebration. Olivia was my height, same medium brown complexion as me and had brown hair down to her shoulders. In my eyes, we could have been twins in another life. She had parents who still lived together and one brother, a real all American family. Her Dad was a deacon in the church and kept her and her family close to God which I really admired about them. I also applauded the fact that her parents were still together and a side of me always wished my parents were still together so I could have a normal family.

Midway through the summer class, I started to feel really sick in the mornings. I'd get up early for class and literally could barely get out of bed. I don't know how I made it to class some days, but I would get there and then be in the nurse's office the whole time, unable to move. One week it was so bad I stayed in bed for a few days, missed school, and just tried to fight what I thought was the flu!

One afternoon my mom came over to visit me because she heard I was not feeling well for a few days so she became concerned. She knew I looked like hell when she saw me and immediately got me ready and took me to the hospital where she worked. The drive to the hospital which was only 15 minutes, felt like a two hour drive because I was so nauseous the whole time. They put me in a bed in the emergency room, took bloodwork from me and ran a bunch of tests. After they finished I fell asleep from exhaustion and dehydration. My mother came back into the area where I was sleeping and shook me awake. She said, "You know what's wrong with you!!!? You are pregnant!! That's why you are feeling like this. You are pregnant!!!" At that point all time stopped. The room got dark and I couldn't grab my bearings. I was woken up out of sleep thinking I was in a dream. Pregnant? How could I be pregnant? What does that even mean to be pregnant? I am too young to get pregnant, right? How does this happen? I just rolled over in my hospital bed and cried, and at that point I wanted to be dead...

She took me home and basically told me not to speak a word of this to anyone, including my father. Later on that week my mom told me she spoke to one of her Dr. friends at the hospital who knew another doctor at Nassau County Medical Center who would perform the procedure...the abortion procedure. Huh? What? I didn't even know what was happening here. I guess that's it, no chance to think about other options, adoption, or having the baby. The decision was made for me and at the time, I didn't realize what this decision was going to do to the rest of my life.

My mother already knew who the father of the baby was even though I hadn't told her. How did she know? Rumors. Neighbors. In essence, everyone knew how sick in love I was with Spencer. I had also never had sex with anyone else. How was I going to tell Spencer? Here's a guy who is messing around with at least two other girls that I knew about and now the girl he's messing with on the down low is pregnant with his baby!

When I got up the nerve to talk to Spencer about this he asked me if I was sure it was his kid. Although he said this in a joking manner, I did not think it was funny at all. I said this was not the time for jokes and he knew it was his kid because I hadn't been intimate with anyone else. I was too scared and too loyal to him to a fault to be having sex with anyone else. He immediately recognized, as my mom had, that the only way out was to have an abortion. In my opinion, although this was a decision that was made for me. I didn't even have a chance to think about it as an option, it was the only option. How could I have a baby at 16 years old?

The days leading up to going to the hospital to have the procedure done were quite strange. It was somewhat of a relief to know why I had been feeling sick for almost two weeks, drained, vomiting daily, with no appetite, losing weight, and having no interest in showering or getting dressed. I was feeling ugly and not sure what was wrong with me. I was 16 years old and now that I knew I was pregnant, it made sense that what I was feeling was all related to this thing happening inside me. I wouldn't even name it a pregnancy or a baby because I was so detached from the process and the understanding of my condition. I only knew the emotion associated with it.

I felt guilty, disconnected, shameful and worthless. All I knew was that Spencer was moving along with his life and I was living in a total hell. The looks I received from my mom and the conversations we had really solidified that feeling. I felt stupid and wanted to say that no one ever had told me about this. I wanted to put the blame on someone else. I was never educated, really educated about the consequences of having sex and the helpless position it puts you in against a boy or a man when you don't abstain or use protection. *I also never understood the long-term consequences these actions would bring to my life and my future. I never saw myself in a futuristic way, never thought of myself as a long-term human being in the bigger picture of life and how I would feel about the guilt that I would carry with me for years into the future.*

On the day of the procedure my mother checked me into the hospital very early in the morning. I remember the long drive with her to Nassau County Medical Center which was really just a few miles down the road from my house, but it felt like the longest drive I had ever taken on a never ending road leading to hell. We didn't speak in the car at all. I was scared, I did not know what to expect, but I knew I would have to stay in the hospital overnight. For a brief moment I had second thoughts about going at all, but ultimately knew this was a done deal. That morning I was settled into a room by myself. It was all white and cold as ice. Before they took me into the operating room I was terrified and worried about what would happen next.

I spoke with Spencer the night before and gave him all the details of where I would be and the time of the procedure, hoping he would have the decency to come and meet me in the hospital. He told me some crock pot story about having to be somewhere with Angela and he didn't think he would make it to the hospital. I was furious, hurt and pissed. I felt betrayed. This person who I had given everything to including my virginity and my soul, was not going to be there for me when I really needed him.

Just as I was heading into the operating room the door to my room opened. I was expecting the porters who would be rolling me out to the operating room, but to my surprise it was Spencer. He showed up at the hospital contrary to what he had said, which gave me a small glimmer of hope about his feelings for me. I was overwhelmed. It was quite uncomfortable because my mother was also in the room with me at the time. She stepped out of the room briefly while we spoke. When she turned around and walked away it was like the air in the room left with her. I had asked Spencer if he'd ever been in this position before, getting a girl pregnant, and he told me no. It was obvious that he was also scared. He was distant to say the least, didn't appear to know what to say or what to do at that moment. I felt nervous for him at a moment when I should have been thinking of myself. The steps I was about to take would likely change my life forever.

Spencer and I exchanged very few words. It was an awkward situation for both of us. Mostly he just stared into space and looked around the room and then looked back at me and attempted to be as kind as he could. He told me he was sorry and that I should call him when I got home tomorrow. Then he headed out to go on with his life outside of that hospital room while I was about to go into this black hole in an operating room that scared the hell out of me. I didn't think I would survive this experience.

Soon after, the attendant came to take me into the procedure room. He was a black male and introduced himself to me as Peter. He asked if I was doing okay and tried to prepare me for where he was taking me and guided me on what turns we were taking in the hallway and into the operating room. Once we arrived, he said he'd be back for me later and gave me a look of assurance and a wink that provided me with a little light of support. The doctor approached and explained what I could expect with the procedure and told me he would be putting a mask over my face to allow the anesthesia to flow through my nose. From there he told me to count back from the number 20. I remember getting to 17 and then it was lights out.

All I know is that the procedure didn't last very long since I don't remember a thing about it. When I got back to the room I had a roommate and, interestingly enough, she was there to have the same procedure as me. This was shocking to me. She seemed a little older than I was. As a result I expected that she might have also been smarter than me to not have been caught in a stupid situation like this. She brought me some relief to know that I was not the only one who had made such a huge mistake. After she left for her procedure I basically slept for the next 24 hours on and off while pondering what I had just experienced. I was mainly relieved to have it over with. I promised myself this would never happen to me again..... ***This experience created a grave in my soul.***

As I settled into school that year I tried to have a new lease on life. Earlier that year, when the New Year turned over into 1986 I made a few New Year's resolutions that included to stop smoking entirely, to concentrate more on my schoolwork, to be more independent and able to make my own decisions, and to be more careful when it comes to choosing my friends and improving the way I act.

I became more engaged with cheerleading and spent a lot of time at the basketball and football games depending on the season. One Saturday in January I practiced cheerleading for the entire day. We were preparing for the Hillcrest High School basketball game at the Nassau Coliseum. The game was mainly designed to be a battle of the cheerleaders. When we got to the coliseum, we practiced in the locker room briefly then hit the floor. We dissed their squad by reading newspapers while they were cheering. Everyone laughed and liked that part. We saw all the hip hop artists of the time perform including Dana Dane, the Force MD's, the Fat Boys and Evelyn Champagne King. Prince Ellie Dee was in our locker room while we were practicing at one point. It was a surreal experience. Spencer and the crew were up there too. He looked fresh in his black leather sheepskin and hat. He was an adult now in my eyes since he was no longer in high school and I attempted to move Spencer out of my head.

I went through a dating period with a boy at school named Mason. I was quite smitten with him for a while. Mason was adorable! He was not that tall but he was muscular, a really good football player, and had Indian looking complexion and dark coolie good hair. He was also popular with the girls. I heard a lot of rumors about him being a player and that he was more focused on running around than getting serious. Although I had heard a lot of rumors about him I was enjoying his company and although it wasn't true love, it felt like we got along really well. He made me think it was all about me, but interestingly enough, I found out about all these other girls he was interested in including a white girl named Grace! I continued to play the game.

I remember the first time we really got together. A bunch of us had cut school and went to hang out down the block at Camilla's house. She lived right on Goodrich St., the same block as the high school. This was so stupid because we could have easily been busted so close to the high school but we cut class anyway.

Back in those days I was always so interested in trying to be committed to a guy and these guys were always interested in something else. Once they got "it" they moved on to the next thing and didn't give a damn about how you felt. With Mason, we went through this on again off again relationship drama. I was stupid to believe he really cared about me when in essence he was only thinking of himself. Being the product of a divorced family made me feel the constant need of having more value in my relationships, and it was important to me to find a long-term and significant connection with someone.

At this time I was dealing with a lot of stress. Since my parents had divorced when I was in 7th grade, I only saw my Mom from time to time. She would pick me up and spend some time with me, but then we were always fighting about something. I just felt like she didn't understand me or really know the pain I was going through. It was strange not having her around on a daily basis like all the other girlfriends I had. They all had their mothers around and I felt motherless. The loss of my mother from the house and the emptiness I always felt without her around full-time made me feel like something was always missing in my life, so I was constantly trying to fill that void. I didn't really have anyone to confide in or to talk to about how I was feeling. I wanted to be able to talk to someone I could trust who wouldn't judge me for my feelings. Girls were always so competitive with each other in high school so you didn't want to share your secrets with them and, if you did, you had to worry that in 10 minutes everyone else would know your business. More times than ever it was within my relationship with boys that I was trying to fill this empty void, hoping that they would love me and give me attention. The attention I missed getting from my mother.

My sister Lillian who is my father's first daughter, often times tried to be the mother figure in my life which was nice, but it wasn't the same although I respected her. I spent a lot of time babysitting her daughter Layla, so she probably felt like we were both her daughters. I could never really talk to her about boys or my problems though partially because of our 20-year age difference and not being sure how she would react to my discussions. I also didn't want her to know that I was sexually active.

During this time it was very difficult to remain focused because peer pressure and being popular was so important to everyone. One minute you were friends with this person and the next minute they were talking about you behind your back and ready to have a fight with you over something stupid and meaningless. I am also shocked when I look back on it now, but we spent a lot of time drinking and smoking weed. It is a mystery how some of us got through high school. I remember one day Hannah (Mason's sister) and I cut 2nd period health class and were looking for some weed to get high. A friend of ours asked me if we had paper (weed rolling paper) and Hannah did so she said we could get down and smoke with her. We got so fucked up. I got kicked out of my Spanish class because I was falling asleep. I failed a social studies test with a 52..**fuck** and never did I stop to think that all this misbehaving would have an effect on my future. There goes my new year's resolution to do better in school. It simply fell by the wayside. For some reason I couldn't stay focused and became so distracted with drugs and alcohol. I just wanted to have fun and not have so many responsibilities.

My mother came to pick me up after school on this particular Friday. I told her I didn't want to spend the night but she made me feel guilty so I went anyway. She had a tendency of saying things to make me feel guilty. She had company that night. Uncle Ronnie and Aunt Erica came over so I assumed she wanted to prove to them that she did spend time with me. I was falling asleep the whole time and completely uninterested in being there. When they left, I crashed out and fell asleep without any questions. I was on the phone at one point with Mason and he asked me to read the love story out loud that he had written about us that he gave me earlier in the day at school. The story was so wacky and non-poetic. I was reading it to him and he was embarrassed because it had some sexual references in it. It was funny though. I was humoring him that the story was funny (but it was kind of corny). I was only happy to see he was thinking about me.

Later that week Tracey told me that Angela and Spencer had broken up. He told her this time it was for real and he took his ring back and everything he had given her. I wanted to believe it but I had heard this all before. I had hopes that if they ever broke up, I could possibly get him back even though he was never really hers. I still loved him, but wondered if he was even interested in me anymore. Day by day things change and you never know what could be in store for you from one day to the next.

I stayed home sick from school the next day, sitting on the orange shag carpet in my living room in front of the television drinking soda and watching All My Children on television. Breaking news came over the TV and they cut the broadcast to the highly anticipated take off of the Space Shuttle Challenger. This was big news because for the first time a non-astronaut civilian woman who was a school teacher had been preparing to take her first trip into space. It was exciting news for our time, so I sat back and waited for the shuttle to take off. Within 73 seconds of the flight taking off as it soared up into the sky, there was an explosion…the spaceship broke apart into what seemed like thousands of pieces and disintegrated in midair, killing all seven crew members. I sat there in disbelief, wondering to myself how life could end so suddenly and unexpectedly. RIP

REGRETS

4

Pomp and Circumstance...Not

It was September of 1986 and finally my senior year in high school! Tracey had graduated that summer and I couldn't believe my time had finally come. It was so important for me to make it to my senior year. This milestone made me feel like I had made it to maturity and could now make my own decisions, adult decisions like dating, choosing a college to go to and going wherever I wanted to go without my father's permission. My brothers, who were four and five years older than me, were always out with their girlfriends, dating and doing adult things. As an example, whenever we went to visit my Mom as a family, they came with their girlfriends. Will had his longtime girlfriend with him and Tony always had someone! Tony was a real ladies man. Both of my brothers were good looking. Will was a little taller than Tony and looked a lot like my mother, more like a coolie with jet black curly hair. Tony looked and acted more like my father; medium build with a short afro. All my girlfriends thought my brothers were cute. At the time I think Tony was dating a beautiful Haitian girl. I couldn't wait until I had the freedom to date and bring my boyfriends to the house like they were allowed to.

I was always rushing to grow up fast. I never really knew why except for the fact that I was the baby and had so many older brothers and sisters that I became tired of watching them live out their adult lives in front of me. At some point in my senior year I began to realize that Spencer was off doing his own thing so I spent my time paying attention to some of the guys in high school who were "feeling me".

Although Mason was still trying to play like he was interested specifically in me, it was David who I became most interested in. Mason and I eventually officially broke up although it was hard to believe we were ever really a couple. He was seeing other people, but he and I were still fooling around, which was a pattern I took on in relationships. I am not sure why I didn't see myself as valuable enough to be in a committed relationship and demand that exclusiveness for myself or maybe in high school it wasn't that important. Maybe I was too young to be committed to one person.

I'd see Mason with other girls and he'd just give me a shameful look. The same thing happened with Spencer. It was like I wasn't respecting myself enough to just be by myself or to ensure that guys respected me if they considered me their girlfriend or to agree openly that it wasn't an exclusive relationship. It appeared difficult to have those conversations in high school. Maybe our brains were not evolved enough to come to terms with those adult decisions.

I don't believe I was the only young girl who went through this. It just felt so good to be liked by a boy that it seemed as if I would do anything to get them to keep liking me. If I loved myself more I would have realized that I was worthy enough to be someone's only girlfriend, and if they didn't value me then I shouldn't be so interested in them.

When I think about David I want to say it was his low key, quiet image that hooked me in the most. David was good looking, very light-skinned with brown curly hair, tall, with a strong build and a smooth style. He played football so he was built and well put together. Once we finally became an item though, it was so difficult for me to figure him out. He was really quiet, so it was hard to understand how he was feeling at times. Personally, I am a much more animated person and needed to have conversations to understand where someone's head was at, particularly someone I am in a relationship with, and so it was difficult at times to relate to him. Even with that dilemma, he had a special place in my heart.

During my senior year in January of 1987, I was having a ton of trouble getting to school on time and I was spending a little bit too much time smoking weed in between classes; sometimes not going to class at all. At one point in the early part of January I was called down to meet with Principal Beyrer about the fact that I was failing gym.

He said based on my lack of physical education credits he was pretty sure I'd be in summer school, but more discussion with administration was to follow. He told me he would let me know the outcome of the discussions in a few weeks. How could I go to summer school in my senior year? That would just be incomprehensible. I didn't think about it much more for a while.

In the early part of January we all made plans to go to a "Classics" game at the Nassau Coliseum. It was a basketball game that happens every year with celebrities and a lot of action. The game started at 11 am on a Sunday and Stella and I got up at the last minute to get going. I met Stella in the 7th grade. She came to our town after living in White Plains for many years. I am not sure exactly how we met, but we hit it off immediately. She used to live over by the 7-11 near Uniondale High School so the back of her house had access to the main road on Front St. We would hang out over her house often since it was walking distance from my house.

Stella had chocolate brown skin, sort of chunky, but the boys always thought she was sexy. She was a very pretty girl with strong, unique features like big brown eyes. Since she came from White Plains, she was not like all the other girls from Uniondale. Like Tracey & Sam, coming from Queens growing up in a different environment than Long Island gave you a unique persona in the neighborhood. She spent a lot of time going back to White Plains because her Dad lived close by there and her Mom moved to

Uniondale after their divorce. I went up there to visit with her a few times. We spent a lot of time with her cousin Skylar who, down the road, ended up getting involved with John, one of Spencer's best friend's at the time. Skylar and John eventually had a daughter together named Savannah. Stella used to dance and spent some time with dance crews from Mt. Vernon and White Plains. She was even friends with Al B. Sure and Heavy Dee & the Boyz who were also from Mt. Vernon.

Stella and I got dressed and walked from her house over to Manor Pkwy. to get Tracey and Sam for the Classics game, but they weren't ready. Stella and I got a little high before we got there so we were still in the mood to keep walking and headed down the block to the Nassau Coliseum. We stopped off at the deli across the street and ended up running into a few of our home girls from high school, Natalie and Hannah. Natalie was Hannah's best friend. Hannah was a beautiful light-skinned girl with hazel eyes. Even though she was Mason's sister, we never, ever talked about him. It was like an unspoken rule between us that he was off limits to our conversations and it was perfect that way.

We eventually met up with Tracey and Sam at the game. We walked around a bit. We were smoking in the seats and left at half time of the last game. Everyone there looked and acted as if they were under the influence of cocaine. We were all bugging out, high and carrying on up in the stands. Girls from all over New York were there and had on their best "stupid fresh gear" including leather Gucci jackets and Mercedes Benz jackets! I was saying to myself, "I need a real job to get some money and get my shit together so I can UP my fashion game". I would say to myself, "Word up!" I really wanted to learn how to handle my life and finances better so I could have money to buy all the nice things I wanted in life.

When I got back to school that week, I noticed I had been thinking a lot about Mason again, even though I was getting friendlier with David. Mason had been acting pretty selfish lately to me. It was almost like I did not exist.

At this time, Olivia and I were going through some bumps in our friendship. We would talk and then get into disagreements here and there. We would not talk for a week and then start talking again. She was spending a great deal of time with Laura, who was originally Stella's best friend. It was like we switched over and Stella took me and Laura took Olivia. I can't help but wonder if I was a little jealous of Laura. Laura was light-skinned, almost white, and with short light brown hair and her body was very fit, muscular but not too muscular. She was always interested in the same guys as me and it seems as if the same guys were interested in her. I feel like a great deal of that was going on in high school, but as a young girl, we girls never realized how disrespectful it was to us that guys were dating around. We just moved on to liking the next guy, then it became a circular process.

I have kept a diary since the 7th grade. Looking back on these times has been somewhat of a trip for me. Some memories you just don't forget, but I am not sure I would have remembered some situations and decisions I made if I hadn't kept track of them by writing in my diary. Stella and I also used to keep notebook diaries with each other. The book was notes we shared throughout the day. Then we'd pass it off to each other as we switched classes. I'd write a letter to her during one period and then pass it along to her and she would do the same the next time she saw me. It was quite intense. Then we would go back and read them to each other. In essence, it was texting before the existence of social media. It goes to show the importance of communication between friends.

Stella and I spent a lot of time together in after school activities. It was cheerleading for me and boosters for her. Boosters were the sexy, cool dancers who made up routines to different songs that we loved during basketball games and half time shows for football. Stella spent our senior year in high school with Dylan who became my best guy friend at the time. Dylan and Mason were best friends as well. We had some interesting times together. Dylan had a smile that went on for days. His light-skinned complexion and character were so sweet and appealing. He was a cool dude who loved to dress and always had jokes to tell. He spent a lot of our senior year teaching me how to drive. As a friend, he was there for me and would also let me cry on his shoulder when I got upset about relationship issues with Mason.

I recall many memories of my senior year, including the details of what was our highly anticipated senior trip in February to the Poconos. Stella and I had been spending a lot of time with Natalie and Hannah. At this time, we were experimenting a lot with smoking weed. There was a group of us who smoked and some of us who didn't. My best friends Olivia and Kennedy were in the "not smoking" crowd. Olivia and Kennedy went to elementary school together and lived on the South side of town. Kennedy was Panamanian and came from a big family of sisters and one brother. Her parents spoke Spanish at home and she also wore a gold tooth which was traditionally a Panamanian thing.

Although I had an alliance to them as my best friends since 7th grade, a bit of separation was created in our senior year based on what types of activities we were into. Since they weren't smokers and Stella and I and others were, we ended up separating from them on several occasions, including during the class trip. Stella and I made the decision that we were going to be roommates with Natalie and Hannah on the high school senior trip and not with Olivia and Kennedy which caused some animosity since we knew they wouldn't want to do the same things we did. It became one of these "mean girls" episodes that you see in a movie with the good girls vs the bad girls. Friendships are really tested in high school and sometimes for no reason at all. If only we were just honest with each other. I think I was afraid to tell them that I wanted to stay with my other friends who were going to do things that they would not be interested in doing, like smoking weed and drinking liquor.

On Saturday night of our senior trip, me, and several other girls spent the night at Stella's house so we could be as close to the high school as possible. This is where we would meet the bus to take us on the senior trip to the Poconos. We drove around Uniondale and were smoking as usual, then returned to Stella's house to chill. We were excited about the next day ahead of us. David and a few of his friends came by also. We stayed up until 5 am which means we never slept. We had planned to wake up by 5 am because there were so many of us to go into the bathroom to get ready for the trip. On Sunday morning we got dressed and arrived at school. Most of the trip I was hanging out with Stella, Natalie, Hannah, Mason and Dylan. The ride was three hours long up into the winding mountains of the Poconos in Pennsylvania. When we finally got there we checked into our rooms and rolled a joint and smoked again. We hung out with the "white girl crew" and then we all got dressed for dinner. I was pretty sure I saw Mason making out with one of the white girls from a distance, but I wasn't confident it was them or that's what I told myself.

We smoked so much weed on this trip that it was ridiculous. This was also the first time that I tried cocaine. I didn't find it to be something that was appealing to me so the try didn't go beyond that. We had received a large enough stash of weed that we were smoking all night. Curfew was at 3 am and we eventually just knocked out. The next morning we got dressed, smoked a joint and went to breakfast. Stella and I attempted to go horseback riding. Stella chickened out and backed off but I ended up going with others on the trail. It was my first time riding a horse and I enjoyed being out there taking on an adventure. Afterwards we smoked another joint and waited for lunch. After lunch we loaded the bus and headed home. It was a simple one day/one night trip, but felt like a lifetime away from home. On this trip I learned a lot about different people and the personalities of my friends and those who I thought were my friends. Although I spent time hanging around the white girls, I had no idea one of them liked the same guy I liked, and obviously had been keeping it a secret. Everything is not always what it seems which makes staying true to yourself so very important and also always trusting your gut.

When we got home, Stella, Dylan, Mason and I spent some time at Dylan's house. Mason and I hadn't really been together for at least two months. At Dylan's house we were just talking and laughing. It was then that I realized he was probably just using me for sex at the time we were intimate but when you are young you don't realize these things at all. You assume people like you for who you are. I don't know, maybe I was wrong. I found out later on in life that Mason had a son with a girl he knew from his hometown. He seemed very distracted with that part of his life which helped me understand a lot more about what he was going through and that I was nothing more than a complication to the situation. I finally opened my eyes and turned my interest away from him altogether with no hard feelings. Sometimes you realize that life puts you on a certain path for reasons you may not learn until later.

A day or so after the trip I was reminiscing about the moment that David and I took some pictures together on the sprawling staircase in the Great Room of the cabin that we all stayed in on the trip. I was starting to feel like he and I were getting closer. Dylan and Stella, on the other hand, had some breakthrough. It seemed as if although she questioned if he was the right guy for her, she continued to play along with him. They would fight on and off and always make up. He was someone that really liked her and cared about her, but she would like him one minute and then the next minute she wasn't sure if she was serious about him. They both seemed to enjoy the game of cat and mouse they played. Their attraction was very strong towards each other.

After the class trip in the early part of February, 1987, Principal Beyrer called me back into his office to confirm that I would have to go to summer school for GYM! The long walk down the hallway into his office with the full length glass mirrors where everyone could see me in the waiting room was embarrassing. Me, "Miss Cheerleader",

"Miss Committed to School Spirit", me "Miss Appearance is EVERYTHING", was not going to be able to graduate. I don't even know how I stayed on the cheerleading squad for the remainder of the year with that doom in my zone. How could I let this happen to me? This was the dreaded payback for not going to class, smoking too much weed, and not doing what I was supposed to be doing. I was completely devastated. Out of all of my friends, this was only happening to me...although others cut class and played around, they were getting it done and planning to graduate and I wasn't.

During this time period Anna's mom got really sick. Anna was one of my good friends on Manor Pkwy. Anna was the girl on Manor Pkwy with the BIG breasts. The guys went crazy over her because her breasts were unusually big for her age. She was a year older than us because she got held back a grade so she was in the same year at school as we were. Anna's mom ended up going into the hospital and eventually slipped into a coma and ended up in critical condition. Anna was very upset and understandably so. She had two brothers who were having a hard time with the whole thing. They lived with their stepfather who they pretty much hated. I could relate to this since my Mom had also re-married and I could not get myself to get along with my stepfather for the life of me. I blamed him for everything from my parent's break-up to my Mom not being with me, etc. If it rained, that was his fault too. You name it and I considered it my stepfather's fault.

Manor Pkwy was a real soap opera station. We had a tight knit group of friends that all hung around together and there were many storylines within the group. Anthony and Jack, my white Italian brothers, lived across the street from Anna. Anthony was the older brother in my grade and we were best friends since the second grade. He and I walked to California Ave. elementary school together practically every day. Their mom passed away also when we were in 6th grade, and I will never forget it because they came to school and took Anthony out of class to tell him the terrible news. We had the best 6th grade teacher ever at that time. Her name was Ms. Massmann. She was a tiny-framed white woman with black curly hair who used to teach us folk songs and how to speak Spanish and sang these songs with us every Friday afternoon. We looked forward to Fridays in Ms. Massman's class. She was an amazing teacher and person. In recent years, Anthony and I were making plans to go visit her for her retirement party and she ended up passing away shortly before the event. We were devastated to receive that news.

It was quite heartbreaking when Anthony was called out of our 6th grade class about the passing of his Mom. The whole neighborhood was saddened by it. A few years later his Dad got remarried and they had a very hard time accepting their stepmom. They had a lot of really loud fights at the house. After a while it became quite common for his Dad to scream so loud you could hear it outside. In the earlier years, when things were more normal, they had two huge Great Dane dogs that the whole neighborhood was afraid of. They were as tall as his Dad when they stood on their hind legs. Some things you just don't forget about your childhood.

A few days later I received the news that Anna's mother had died. That shit hit me like a ton of bricks! I cried so hysterically that they had to send me home from school. I tried to get Tracey and Sam to come with me to Anna's house to offer my condolences, but they wouldn't at that time so I went alone. They did eventually come over for a little while to support her in her time of mourning. I cried with Anna a little and then we all just sat around spending some time together. I smoked a blunt with Anna's boyfriend and left their house around 10:30 pm. I still couldn't believe that Anna's mother was gone but couldn't help but feel a little more connected to her. Now we both would not have our mothers living at home with us although under very different circumstances.

The soap opera continues....there were two sisters who lived nearby who both hated me because of an incident that happened with a guy who was the older sister's boyfriend at the time. It was his fault, so I don't know why they hated me. In essence, I got drunk one Christmas Eve at a friend's house with a few older guys, including Olivia's older brother. I had so much to drink that one of the boyfriends of the sisters took advantage of me and forced me to kiss him. All I remember is doing it and shortly after throwing up all over the place. His girlfriend found out and tried to blame me as if I was a "home-wrecker". I didn't really care about that because I know I was not in my right mind. I was literally taken advantage of by him. After that I never trusted any of them again and realized how important it is to watch how much you drink and who you hang around with because men can take advantage of you if you are not careful #metoo.

From time to time, I kept going back in my head about my feelings for Mason and how bad I wanted to talk to him, but I refused to call him since I was hurt by our current distance. He knew my number. I had no idea why I was thinking about him and stressing myself out. If he wasn't worried about me, why should I be worried about him? This is bit of the tragedy of my life story. I am always worrying about those who are not treating me well and doing everything in my power to make them like me more. I don't know what this weakness is about in my psyche, but it is something that was deeply ingrained in my thinking process as a young woman. There was some strong desire for me to be liked and not rejected. The experience of losing my mom and her moving out as a result of my parent's divorce was a strong form of rejection for me. As a result of this thinking I also felt the need to be able to have things so that I could take care of myself and not need things from other people. This way I could limit my fear of rejection.

Ever since I was young I remember always having a job. My first job was at Burger King in Roosevelt Field mall. I recall only working there for a short time and then getting fired because I gave some guy a free soda, by mistake. I didn't even know the guy so it's not like I was trying to hook him up or anything, I was just young and didn't know any better. I also spent some time working at Bits and Bytes which was the Café at Hofstra University. All the local kids worked there including my brothers and Spencer. I didn't really enjoy working around food because I always came home smelling really bad and feeling dirty. I also spent some time working at Marshall's, which was a lot more fun because I loved shopping and seeing all the new clothes coming in. I spent the longest amount of time in my senior year working at Macy's. I was positioned in the women's section and spent a good amount of time in the fitting room. Thinking back now, I am not proud of it, but I even made out with a couple of pieces using my five-finger discount (meaning I didn't pay for them). Of course, it was stuff I could not afford, like Adrienne Vittadini sportswear suits, nice career sweaters and skirts. I do regret that.

This experience proved to me that I always knew I had to do whatever I could to support myself and have my own money. It was really important to me. My father always complained of not having a lot of money. "Money doesn't grow on trees" he would say. He was very tight with so many things around the house, including the electricity. We always had to turn off the lights and he wouldn't turn the heat up past 67 degrees so we had to wear extra clothes if it was cold. We had a washing machine in our house that you had to feed quarters into to make it work. I think he really did that for my brothers because he gave me the key to clean out the quarters and I used them to wash our clothes since I was doing all the laundry including his underwear. I was just his little wife at the time. When I wanted to go out and enjoy myself, I couldn't unless all the chores in the house were done. I did find the time to go out though, whenever I could, even if I had to sneak out.

I was so excited when David asked me to go to the prom with him. I immediately said yes and started to plan the entire ensemble. I wore a light blue lace dress that Will's girlfriend at the time made for me. I had a beautiful asymmetrical haircut, which was in at the time and had my nails done long and perfectly manicured. My Mom came over to help get me ready. After I was dressed, the classic stretch white Mercedes Benz (with David in it) came to pick me up. It was so gorgeous! David wanted to go to the prom in style and wanted nothing but the best. He brought me a lovely corsage and we took pictures in front of the house with all of my friends and neighbors gathered around. He was clearly uncomfortable with all the attention. I felt like a princess that night. Unfortunately, David got so drunk that once we left the after parties we checked into a motel in Queens near JFK airport where he passed out. I told my father I was staying at Stella's house because he never would have understood why I stayed in a motel. I didn't even get a kiss good night from David. Most high school seniors get lucky on prom night but I ended up pretty unlucky, and disappointed. The next day we went to Six Flags Great Adventure in New Jersey, which was the cool thing for high school seniors to do at that time. We were so exhausted when we got back home. That night, we snuggled up, got close and shared a sweet moment of intimacy at his house. No one else was home and we had a good time. He made up for prom night that night.

The best news ever in my senior year was finding out that I was accepted to Virginia State University! Wow! I was going to college! I always knew I would go, I just didn't know where. I couldn't believe that I was going to be moving away from home to go to college. By then it was confirmed that I would not be graduating with my class. Based on all the days that I skipped gym class, swimming, specifically, I was considered incomplete, and there would be no time to make it up. Since Uniondale High School had an Olympic size swimming pool in our building we were required to take swimming as a class for an entire quarter. I barely went to class and resented the fact that I had to get my hair wet every other day and still function as a "popular" student who looked like somebody trying to get attention from boys. What a fool I was! Instead, I spent time smoking weed, cutting classes and not recognizing the importance of following through with my responsibilities. It all led to a moment of embarrassment. I look back now and see it wasn't worth it at all. The good news in all of this is that I was able to go to the prom and had been on the senior trip even though I was not going to graduate, and this was the most important event of the year. I often wondered if they counted my credits late on purpose, or the administration didn't want to ruin my entire senior year, but either way, it taught me a very important message about staying focused and getting shit done. Yet,

I only missed graduation which was the most important part of my senior year...

I was one of a small handful of people who were not in attendance at my Class of 1987 high school graduation. The day it took place, at the time it was happening, I stayed in bed with the covers over my head crying my eyes out. I will always remember this as the most painful disappointment that I could have ever had. Even though this was something I had control over in my life. I screwed it up. I am sure it was a real disappointment for my parents also. I vowed to myself that day, to not ever let laziness get in the way of my successes. Later on that evening, David picked me up and we went out. It was somewhat awkward that he graduated and I didn't. I wonder if he thought less of me as a result. If he did, he never showed it and I appreciated him so much for that.

I spent the summer of 87 in summer school....for GYM. What a dumbass. I guess it wasn't all bad since Sam was in the class with me. Not so bad for her though, since she was a junior and had one more year of high school to go to and another year to make it right. I always tried to look at the bright side of everything but in this case it was a disappointment that I held in my heart and soul. Either way, the good news is that at the end of this rotten summer filled with gym class, I would be heading off to college in Virginia.

5

Virginia State University:
Here We Go Again

I was super excited to be preparing to go to college. Stella and I went on tour to a few colleges earlier in the year but ultimately selected Virginia State University in Petersburg, VA as our favorite and first choice. We both received our acceptance letters at around the same time. When my letter came we were in my bedroom. I read it out loud. "Congratulations you have been accepted to Virginia State University!" We started screaming and jumping up and down and hugging each other.

We selected Virginia State for a few reasons. First of all it was very far away! I personally could not wait for my freedom from my father. My father was so strict and the thought of no longer having to be a maid was delightful. Secondly, Virginia State was a popular school well-known as a party school and, of course, we wanted to have some fun. Finally, the school was considered a historically black college. Historically black colleges and universities (HBCUs) in the

United States were established before the Civil Rights Act of 1964 with the intention of primarily serving the African-American community. This was because the overwhelming majority of predominantly white institutions of higher-learning disqualified African Americans from enrollment during segregation. The thought of going to a historically black college made me feel like I was connecting more closely with my black history.

My Dad and his girlfriend at the time took us down for our last visit to the school late in the summer of 1987. It was a long ride on I-95 but well worth it. We stopped in D.C. and visited the Lincoln Memorial and a few other historical sites. On the way back, I remember being in the car and hearing on the radio that a member of the group KRS-1, also known as Boogie Down Productions (BDP), was shot and killed. His name was DJ Scott La Rock. It was so unusual to hear that, very sad, but a memory I will never forget. BDP was one of my favorite hip hop groups of all time. Some of their songs were "Criminal Minded", "South Bronx" and the "Bridge is Over" to name a few. Their rap style was enveloped in education and mindfulness way before the #staywoke movement was introduced. In my opinion, they helped originate this movement of awareness of issues concerning social and racial justice through their rap words, artistic videos and performances.

David and I spent most of the summer hanging out together because we knew we were separating in September with each of us going to different schools and different states. He was going to play football for the University of Connecticut. I was pretty sad we were separating, but very excited to be moving away from home with my best friend. I swear, for the entire summer, David and I spent what felt like every day together. After summer school where I was taking gym class, we went to the movies and to the beach, but it also felt like we spent a great deal of time having sex. It seems as if we were doing it almost every other day. One of the interesting things though, is I don't remember us ever using protection in the way of condoms.

I went with his mom to visit him in college since he left ahead of me, and during the entire drive I bragged to his mom about what a great guy he was. By the time summer ended and we both went away to college, he and I went our separate ways. I don't recall us officially splitting up, but when I arrived at college with Stella, it was like a whole new world.

Upon arrival at college in Petersburg, Virginia Stella and I met several friends that we ended up connecting with almost immediately. We met a beautiful girl named Ruby in the financial aid line on our first day on campus. She was light skinned, tall, super pretty with long brown hair. We found out immediately that her parents were Jamaican, like ours, so we immediately hit it off talking patois and making fun of our amazing heritage. She took us back to the dorm to meet her best friend, Lydia, who she had come to college with from Brooklyn. Lydia had a very spunky personality. She had short darker brown hair, brown complexion and a mouth like a fire cracker. She always had jokes and was sarcastic as hell. She used to walk around school with a radio box the size of a medium sized suitcase that we played music from all the time. We all ended up in the same dorm so we became inseparable. We named our small group Six Pack and a Pint since one of our friends was very tiny. Wherever we went, we did it together. We created our own on campus gang.

On campus I caught the attention of a guy named Caleb from Hempstead who was completely smitten with me. Caleb was tall with a lighter complexion and nice build. After meeting him I later found out that he came to school with Trina, his high school girlfriend. She and I had a slight resemblance to each other, or so people said, so I guess I can see why Caleb was interested in me.

They came to the college tour together in their junior year. Stella remembered that and reminded me of it when she ran into him on campus. They remembered each other when they met again. Caleb was friends with two guys named Jaxon and Eli. Jaxon was so good looking. He had looks we considered coolie; Indian skin, brown complexion, and dark curly hair. He was adorable. Eli was not bad looking either; a little on the heavier side, but not too crazy. They were all joined at the hip as well. Where you saw one, you saw the others. We named their crew Chaos. They were always out having fun, causing trouble wherever they went. Caleb and I were becoming close pretty quickly. He was fighting with his ex-girlfriend Trina every chance they could, and she, from what I understood, wanted to fight me.

After we spent a month settling into college life, homecoming came around. It was actually scheduled on the same day as my birthday, October 10th, 1987. It was going to be a great weekend because my whole family was coming to town including my best friends, Tracey, Sam, Olivia, and so many more. When they arrived from New York after the long road trip no one could find me because I had spent the night in Caleb's dorm room. I woke up in a daze, completely forgetting it was my birthday and that I had such a great weekend ahead of me. Stella called me on the dorm phone and shocked me out of my moment of slumber to tell me my family had arrived. I hustled to my room which was on the other side of campus and jumped all over everyone who was there to see me. We had a full weekend of parties, music, food, dancing and fun. At the end of the weekend, I was so sad to see everyone go.

During this time I was in a really confused state about my love for David and this new crush I was slowly moving towards with Caleb. He was in my room a lot and I spent a lot of time in his, but I continued to feel as if he and Trina still had something going on even though it was apparent they also had great hatred for each other.

At one point early in the fall I started to get really sick. It was sickness I remembered very well. It was not that long ago, only two years, since I'd gotten pregnant with Spencer's child and eventually had my first abortion. For several days I could not keep my food down. But because I was smoking so much weed at the time, I would feel sick, smoke a joint, and then get hungry all over again. It's a symptom of being under the influence of weed that we called the munchies. I'd get up the urge to eat, but then the next day feel sick and vomit, and then the cycle would start all over again. I ended up getting so sick at one point that my dorm friend Clara took me to the infirmary. That's where I found out the hurtful truth. I was pregnant again, and I was devastated.

At this point I'd been having sex with David throughout the entire summer until we left each other for college. After coming to college, I became physically intimate with Caleb at the beginning of October. When I found out I was pregnant, I did not do the math to determine who the father of the child was, I only made assumptions, and at the time, I did not know for sure who the father was.

Trina found out I was pregnant at some point (I have no idea how – I believe Caleb told her) because he was so excited that he had been with me and possibly made this happen, but she shut him down very quickly by accusing him of being sterile and not able to have a child. Was he lying to himself that this was his doing to feel more like a man? In any event, he followed through with assuming all along that it was his child. I wasn't so sure. During this time, David and I were separated but talked on and off, and attempted to give the relationship another try since I still had feelings for him. The fact that it was a long distance relationship did not help. The freedom we had and the many new people we were meeting on campus made it hard for either of us to trust each other. I knew though that I cared about him. I just did not think he was the man for me long term. We were too different. He was always so respectful of me, though, so I always appreciated him for that.

For a variety of reasons I made up my mind that I was going to have another abortion. One, I did not know if the baby was Caleb's or David's at the time. Two, in my eyes I was just too young to have a baby at the age of 18. Three, I could barely take care of myself much less another person. I was smoking weed and drinking alcohol on a very heavy basis. I was clearly addicted. This, in fact, was something very dangerous as I think back now on my health and how I was treating myself while carrying a child. It was unacceptable behavior.

Once I made up my mind to have the abortion, I needed to find the cash to get the procedure done. I left Virginia to go back home during the Thanksgiving holiday and had so many conflicts I was unable to have the procedure done at that time. Against my better judgment I ended up going back to Virginia without doing the procedure. More time passed and I was getting further and further along.

It was getting close to the Christmas holiday and I was practically losing my mind with sickness, depression and fear. I was close to the end of the first trimester of pregnancy. On December 19th of 1987, while preparing to go home for the holidays, I heard through the grapevine that Spencer had a baby girl with a girl named Diana who he started dating right before I left for college. I wrote a note in my diary that said, "Spencer had his first baby girl today, the one who lived!" Once again, I was devastated by this news, but not devastated and stupid enough to also have a baby out of anger and jealousy when all of the other odds were against me.

While in New York during the Christmas holiday I went to the doctor for a checkup to prepare for the procedure. On one occasion I got there too late and they would not see me. On another occasion I was too far along and they would not take me and referred me to another doctor. At that point I was wondering what was really going to happen to me since so much time was passing. I ended up going back to school, I continued to be sick, and missed classes almost daily. Some days I could barely make it out of bed at all. I was throwing up so often that I only had enough energy to walk to class, if at all, go in and take a test, and then return to my room. I'd go back to bed and hide under the covers. I became comfortable with hiding under the covers. It seemed to be where I did my best work...

I was thoroughly ill, confused and depressed. I felt like God had given up on me and had plans to ruin my life for getting myself into this mess again. I ended up going back home again sometime in January because everyone at school (especially my close friends) seemed very concerned about me. My mother caught on to what was wrong with me and once again had to check me into the hospital. This time she and Daddy's girlfriend at the time were in on it together. Due to the fact that my pregnancy was so far along, I had to get more sensitive care. Once I arrived at Hempstead Medical Center I was checked in and given meds immediately to induce the labor to deliver and abort the baby. When the nurse took my initial patient information, vitals and all, she asked me how old I was. I told her 18 years old. She said wow and you're 18 weeks pregnant. With a smug look of disdain, she said, "Thank God you are not 19 or 20 years old!" meaning if that were the case I'd be much farther along if the pregnancy timeline aligned with my age in weeks.

I just put my head down in shame and for a good two hours my mother cursed me out, berating me about doing this again after what I'd been through before. I didn't know what to say. I had no answers. I was feeling so dumb, ignorant, and angry with myself. The fact that my decision to allow myself to have sex and once again not use protection and put myself in a desperate and dangerous position was killing me inside. My father's girlfriend stood quiet. It was obvious she was sad for me but didn't know what to say since she was just my father's girlfriend. She probably felt that my mother was doing a great job cursing me out all by herself.

After a little while they left me alone in the hospital room. My room had a direct view of Front St. I could practically walk home, and I wanted to. I lay in the cold, lonely hospital bed and looked out the window and just waited for the medicine to kick in. Late in the night I started having the worst pains I have ever felt in my whole life.

Apparently this is what labor felt like. I was given meds to start the labor process to give birth and the pain was unbearable. My insides felt like I had been kicked 1000 times and there was no cure in sight to make it better.

After about an hour of that tremendous pain I felt the urge to use the bathroom, to actually "blast off" and when I sat down on the toilet, that's when it started to happen. I didn't have to force it or push at all, slowly but surely this mound of human matter came out of my vagina and into the toilet. I began to cry uncontrollably as I pressed the red emergency button on the hospital cord and the nurse came rushing in. She tried to calm me down. After a few attempts I slowed my heavy crying to just sobbing and eventually just tears dropped while she removed the embryo from the toilet. It was not alive. I'm sure the medication that they gave me ensured that this was not going to be a healthy delivery.

The next day I was no longer the same. This experience put the worst taste in my mouth, mind, and body. I didn't believe I could ever lose this grave feeling. **I had clearly developed another GRAVE IN MY SOUL.** I was mad at the world. I was mad at Caleb even though deep down I knew it was not his child. He knew he was having sex with me so I felt he should have been there for me and he wasn't. He took a hands-off approach and financially did not want to help me. He literally shunned me during those months I was pregnant. I was mad at David because just maybe he knew the truth that this was his baby, but because he was mad at me for hooking up with Caleb, he could barely face me. I could hardly blame him for how he felt. I just felt so alone in the world from an experience that hadn't happened to me just by my own actions. I didn't get myself pregnant! I knew I was never going to be the same after this moment in time.

When I went back to school I swore off Caleb entirely. He tried to contact me on several occasions. I refused to take his calls or see him. I asked a few guys that I knew who were familiar with the situation to keep him away from me and if that meant to physically harm him, they were ready for that and I was okay with it. He continued to try for a little while to get through to me and then gave up after seeing how difficult it would be for me to give in. When my mind is made up, I am done. I never wanted to see him ever again... and I didn't. David, on the other hand, did give me money towards the procedure. He came to my house and brought it and we had a brief talk that was awkward at the time since we knew this was a bad situation to be in. Although he and I didn't get back together, I felt that in the end he knew the truth. Based on the timing, it was his child, and I do believe he still cared about me. It was my responsibility to take care of myself. I was the one in control and the one responsible for ensuring I protected myself, and I didn't do it. But in the end I did what I thought I had to do to protect myself and my future even though it felt awful and still does.

6

The Business

After this very emotional experience that was the second biggest regret of my life, the summer of '88 came and went quickly. As the second year of college rolled around it was time to get my mind right and pay more attention to my school work. I went back to college with the hope of reassessing my reasons for going away to school in the first place and tried to get focused. I had been spending too much time on boys and all the foolishness that comes with them and not staying focused on important goals like my education. I didn't do that well the first year at Virginia State. I had failed a few classes and was preparing to try and make it better this time around, but it didn't look very promising since a whole new saga was beginning that started with many of my friends leaving college after the first year to go back home and new friends coming into the mix.

The landscape had changed at school. My Brooklyn crew, Ruby and Lydia, had both decided to leave Virginia State after the first year. They didn't enjoy it very much and they were homesick for their cool town of Brooklyn. When they left, the craziest thing happened. Tracey and Sam came to meet me and Stella at school and started to go there with us. Now Manor Pkwy had literally transported itself to Petersburg, Virginia. I had a feeling this was not going to be a good idea and of course, I was right. All of the craziness continued in the worst way because Tracey and Sam had their own apartment off campus when they started school and it was like being in their basement on Manor Pwky all over again, but this time with no parents in sight. Believe it or not, after doing the math, it was cheaper to have your own place off campus than it was to live on campus. Many of us picked up on that after the first year of college out of state. This ended up being a trend for many students who lived in the area. If your parents were willing to see the value of paying less while forgetting their many concerns of the concept of young adults having their own pads far away from home, it was a win-win.

Towards the end of the first year at Virginia State I met a guy from the Bronx named Wayne who showed a great deal of interest in me. Since I was so caught up in the David and Caleb saga, I was not interested in getting serious with any other new guy right now. With that said, he was definitely also not my type. He was on the shorter side, closer to my height or slightly taller, dark-skinned, with strong features, stocky and built like a soccer player. I had always been attracted to light skinned guys. He had a crew of people he hung around with on campus, most of who were also from the Bronx. He came to college with his best friend Leo. A friend of mine named Riley who I had met in our first year started to form a relationship with Leo during the same time period I met Wayne. They quickly became an item.

Riley and I shared the same dorm building in our first year. She was a pretty girl, light-skinned and chunky. She came to Virginia State from Harlem. She was so cool, and wore nothing but Reebok Classics. She had them in every color. She wanted me to get to know Wayne better because he was best friends with Leo and it was an opportunity for us all to hang out together. It started to morph out that way. Wayne was very nice to me. He always gave me money to buy things, like groceries, and then he'd ask me and my friends to cook dinner for him and his friends. In essence, we ended up getting closer and closer over time and spending a lot of time together. Eventually I realized where all the money, cars and more were coming from; drug deals. I didn't really like the idea, but I tried to ignore it as much as possible. That didn't last very long.

Wayne and I started to get into a close and very deep and heated relationship. We were spending every waking moment together. I spent the night at his place a lot. He ended up with an apartment off campus very early on that he and Leo shared together. I started to learn about the "ins and outs" of his business, the drug business. He and his boys often went to New York to collect "work" and bring it back to Virginia and sell it through individuals that were working on the street. After a while this was a routine process. Sometimes I went with them and took the trip to New York to get out of Virginia since I at times was also homesick. Tracey went with me a few times. She was more experienced with this work than I was; especially since she had been around her father's business in Long Island. I was always pretty nervous about it all and hoped that one day Wayne would make enough money to give it up altogether. He had two girls working with him, Mackenzie and Delilah. Mackenzie was cool. She was a real gangster girl, ride or die for her boys. Mackenzie had a light brown skinned complexion. She and Riley were really close because Mackenzie also spent a lot of time with Leo. She would always be running around with them, doing errands, working in the street, etc. They treated her like one of the guys. Delilah, on the other hand, was not so cool with me. I never trusted her. She was one of those pretty, light-skinned girls who I felt had a crush on Wayne, or maybe they had something going on. She was Puerto Rican, kept a shorter haircut styled in a bob, and was a little taller than me. I am pretty sure they had a relationship behind my back, but I never really knew for sure. One time I went to NY for the weekend without Wayne and came back to Virginia and showed up at his apartment very early in the morning and they were both asleep on the bed, fully clothed, but obviously that did not look right to me. I was pissed. She ended up leaving and he and I fought about it and, of course, he claimed nothing was going on. I said yeah, okay, and left it alone.

Our lives were full of chaotic adventures. One night Wayne and I and a few other people went out to eat and to a movie. On the way home after we left the movies I was driving and got into an altercation with a man on the highway. I cut him off by accident. He was really mad. As I got onto I-95 from Richmond, he started to sweat me on the highway and tried to chase me down. I was a little scared and didn't want him to catch up with me for fear of what could happen if we came face to face with him. At the same time, I felt Wayne loved the chase and didn't seem to mind if I kept driving faster. I ended up doing at least 90 mph on I-95 and as we sped closer to the toll booths I practically skidded into them. The police/5-0 pulled over both our cars as we pulled past the toll booth. I told them my side of the story, that I cut him off by accident and that he chased me down the highway. Although I was fearful of him catching me, Wayne was egging me on in the car the whole time to make sure he did not catch up to us. The peer pressure was on to not be caught. The police gave me a summons and I had to go to court about a month later. When I eventually did show up to go to court, the judge gave me a fine for travelling 50 miles over the speed limit. I ended up getting put in a holding cell because Wayne didn't have enough money on him at the time to get me out. He had to go all the way to Petersburg from Richmond to get the balance of the money, and I stayed in the holding cell until he returned several hours later. That was one of the scariest things that had ever happened to me. I didn't like that feeling of being confined in the cell with no ability to get out. I don't want anything like that to ever happen to me again. At that point Wayne saw me as his ace, down with the team, but I wasn't sure where our relationship would go from there. It seemed to have started out on a risky path. One I wasn't sure I was ready to go down.

Wayne and I fought on an off. He was beginning to learn that I was nothing but a loyal girl from Long Island and not a girl who runs around looking for trouble and materialistic things. He is the one that bought me things, Gucci pocketbooks, Michael Jordan sneakers and anything that seemed appealing to him for me. He treated me kindly and more or less worked towards us becoming what I thought would be an exclusive relationship. Once we started dating, his friends started to realize we were becoming an item. I remember one of his friends once saying I only wanted him for his money and that Wayne should go with a girl who really cared about him (referring to Delilah). Of course Wayne says he said that because he was drunk. But I was pissed. I absolutely did not want him for his money but he offered this lifestyle to me to prove in a way that he could take care of me. He thought because of that, he could also treat me a certain way as if to keep me on one side of the tracks, while his other "friendships" within his work were on the other side.

His friends spent a lot of time at the house bottling their work and this could take hours in the middle of playing cards, drinking, smoking weed, counting money, etc. All along, I knew Wayne was probably still in a relationship with Delilah. I hated the ground she walked on. I didn't want to see her in my presence, ever, but she always turned up somehow. Eventually, our relationship became so serious we were inseparable. I went to New York with him often, most times not seeing my family. Since all his work was uptown, in the city, there was never enough time to make it all the way onto the LIE or Grand Central Pkwy to the Cross Island Parkway to the Southern State Pkwy to go around my way. It was just too far out of the way. Every now and again, though, I took the car and left him uptown while I made a brief visit to Long Island on my own.

Wayne had so much going on. One of the exciting things alongside his "business" was the social gatherings and really huge parties he and the team threw. This lifestyle was one busy event after another. This is when I met the World Famous DJ Kid Capri aka Pooch. Wayne, Leo and the crew grew up with Kapri in the Bronx on Kingsbridge Terrace. He was a cool dude. He was light skinned, really light, and looked like he had to be mixed with something other than black. His hair was dark and curly and a little coarse. I found out how mixed he was when one day Wayne brought me to Kid's house on Kingsbridge Terrace where I met his mother. His mother was full blown white, Italian, with really long hair. It was funny to see Kid interact with his Mom since he was so street and down to earth and she was this very white woman, completely hip to his fun and games. You can tell she loved him and was very proud of him. I never met his father, but I assumed he was black. Anyway, Kid became the big deal on the campus at VSU at these really big parties and there would be tons of people there. The best way to describe these events was as gym jams since they were usually held on campus at the school gym or other large venue.

Kid came to Virginia and did parties for us three or four times during the year. The parties were the best parties ever. Kid was an amazing DJ. He was known for playing the best hip hop and old school songs and using techniques to spin and change the records quickly while doing tricks to make the music sound like it was repeating and scratching and starting over again in a way that made hip hoppers and lovers of music go crazy. When you heard his music, you would scream and dance like it was the best thing you had ever heard in your life.

At the same time, we used to hang out with the brothers Aaron and Damian Hall who also spent some time at Virginia State. They used to sing at the talent shows and eventually became a popular R&B group. Damian was a student there, but his brother Aaron was not. Once or twice the girls and I danced with them as back up dancers with Damian and his other on campus partner and eventually he and his brother became the famous group "Guy". Stella dated one for a little while until the group started traveling and gaining popularity. There were rumors that he was dating other people, and he had been traveling all over and it just became too difficult to carry on a long distance relationship. I know she was hurt. I came to realize that men can be so hurtful to women at times, and I always wondered why.

My 19th birthday rolled around on 10/10/88. A day or two before, my Dad came to visit our house in Petersburg with my brother Tony and his girlfriend at the time. My father and I often fought and then made up but it really felt good to have my Dad and brother come and visit me. I showed them around Virginia, took them to the campus and to the mall and let them see what the neighborhood was like. My Dad bought me this beautiful coat while he was visiting, which was so unusual to me since he was so frugal and never thought many purchases were necessary. The act of gifting this coat to me was of huge value since I know he spent his money very thoughtfully. It felt so great to have familiar faces in my home away from home, especially since Virginia seemed like such a foreign place for me at times.

The Ku Klux Klan still marched in the downtown Virginia area in those days. That was not something you see at all in New York. They marched in small groups with full garb inclusive of robes and white hoods with cutout holes for eyes, noses and mouths. It was clear they did not want to be recognized as white supremacists. The majority of Petersburg was white. I always wondered whose idea it was to drop an all-black college into the center of it. As New Yorkers, we turned a blind eye to this fight in southern Virginia at that particular time. Although we recognized the tragedy of what the Klan stood for and that they were still marching; it was on such a low scale that it was often ignored. With that said, it makes me wonder if we should have done more to respond to their marching. At the time, selfishly, I was happy to have my close friends and family there with me and that is all.

On the morning of my birthday, I woke up around 3:30 AM. Wayne woke up too, wished me a happy birthday and then we both went back to sleep. I woke up again around 8 am to a cloudy day. When I got up, I brought him some Nyquil because he was not feeling well. Then I left the house, went to my gym class, came home, and went back to sleep. Wayne was walking out when I woke up again around 2pm. I got dressed quickly and he dropped me off on campus so I could take a Science test. Campus was only a short ride away so it was easy to get to and from there from my apartment. I had a two bedroom main floor apartment that Stella and I shared together. She had her room in the back on the right and mine was up front on the left once you walked in the front door and past the foyer. The rooms were pretty large. We had a huge kitchen where Stella and I often spent time cooking and having a cocktail, talking and laughing about all of our shenanigans.

After class, Leo and Mackenzie took me to Webster Court where they lived. I thought Wayne might be mad because he said he would come and get me, but he hadn't come yet and it wouldn't have been the first time he stood me up. Eventually he showed up and we went back to my house. I was expecting Tracey and Sam to stop by, but by 6 pm, they had still not arrived. I was starting to worry and was actually getting pissed that no one remembered or even wanted to celebrate my birthday with me. I felt completely ignored. Riley had come in the house and left some of our other friends in the car. I thought to myself, wow, they couldn't even come in and wish me a happy birthday?! In my disappointment, I sped off in Wayne's Red Pathfinder to go get a bag of weed. I came back, laid out the weed on the table, pulled out the seeds and proceeded to roll the joint and then smoked it all by myself. Wayne walked by and saw me smoking and took two tokes then he fell asleep. At that point I had a few cocktails by myself. I was really angry that Tracey and the others didn't come over. I started to get very emotional with the liquor and weed in my system and just started to cry. I had a brief "in my feelings" weeping moment, where I was feeling sorry for myself that no one cared enough about me to even say happy birthday. An old friend of ours from NY that Tracey used to date called and said he was coming through town and was going to take a cab from Richmond which I thought was a little unusual. I wondered why he was coming to town.

Later in the evening, Wayne took me out to eat at Annabelle's which was an Italian restaurant just outside of Petersburg. When we got back home he ran some line on me about needing to pick up work from Tracey and Sam's house which he sometimes kept there and asked if I wanted to come with him. I really didn't want to go with him because I was mad at the world over at Tracey and Sam's house but I was not going to stay in the house by myself on my birthday so I said yes even though it wasn't really what I wanted to do. He asked two of his friends to come along.

When we got to Tracey and Sam's house we went in through the back door which wasn't that uncommon. That was at times the main entrance of the house that everyone used. When we got inside I almost had a heart attack when everyone jumped out and said "Surprise and Happy Birthday!" There were like 30 people there. I was so shocked they had surprised me with a birthday party. I should have known better that something was going on. I was immediately overcome with joy. It felt so good to know that my friends cared about me enough to throw me a surprise party. They did a great job of keeping it a secret, too. To the point of me wondering if I even had good friends at all. Once I said hello to everyone and thanked them for coming, we all got so drunk and wasted. The entire house was filled with smoke from all the weed burning up in there. It was a good night.

The next day after coming down from the high of my surprise party, we heard some bad news. Leo and his partner were taken off the yard by the police. They also searched Mackenzie's house and arrested her for possession of drugs. Everyone was on high alert because clearly they would soon be looking for Wayne. At that point the team was paranoid about every move they made. We waited in the house all night to see what was going on and what word was coming from the streets. The streets were talking and they said the police had been searching around a few of the locations that they were used to going to around the way including Webster Court where Leo and Wayne lived. Wayne and their crew made the decision that Wayne was going to have to leave Virginia to hide out. The next day, Wayne left on the bus and went back up north to NY; it was the best way for him to get out of town unnoticed.

A few weeks later Stella and I went to see Mackenzie in jail. She had lost a lot of weight and had been looking very tired, but tried to seem strong like everything was okay. It could not possibly be okay when she was in a Virginia jail facing charges of drug possession! This worried me a lot. My biggest fears for this team were coming to fruition. This could have been any one of us at any time being followed, watched, pulled over or arrested. This is the part of the lifestyle that really scared me. It made me want out of this life.

I made plans to go home for the weekend to spend some time with Wayne. When I arrived on Friday afternoon he met me at the train station. We drove to Sunrise Cinemas movie theatre in Valley Stream to see Halloween, and a big fight broke out. After the weekend ended, I took the train and went back to school. I missed the first two trains because it was difficult saying goodbye to Wayne. I hated that he would not be coming back with me. I finally jumped on the 4:30 pm train to get back to my school business in Virginia.

The Christmas holiday came and I spent most of the time with Wayne in NY. I headed back to Virginia for my second semester of my second year of college in mid-January. Out of nowhere, I was starting to feel sick again. This feeling was a familiar feeling I had felt before. I was nauseous, extremely overtired, irritable and lacking an appetite. I had recently started birth control pills at the recommendation of Planned Parenthood, so I assumed it was the pill that made me ill. However, upon taking a home pregnancy test my ultimate suspicions were confirmed. Apparently this pill method of birth control did not work for me because once again, the nightmare that I kept reliving was happening again. It felt like the movie Groundhog Day where a cynical TV weatherman finds himself reliving the same day over and over again. For the third time, I ended up pregnant. I must have started the pill too late while being sexually active too early. Once again I was in the dilemma where I had to make the decision to possibly abort another baby! Could I really be facing this dilemma again, and right now, along with everything else that was going on? They say the third time is the charm. I just couldn't do it again...

LESSONS

7

Motherhood

At this point I realized it was time for me to step up regardless of what was going on and to prepare myself to make what would be the toughest decision of my life. I won't necessarily say "do the right thing" because the choice to have an abortion or put a child up for adoption is not a right or wrong thing in my opinion. Although many have their own opinions on this, a decision to be pro-life or pro-choice should never be taken lightly, and people should not be judged for their decision to choise. I made the decision that I was going to become the mother to a child. I had so many regrets from my past two decisions to abort, including the moral decision but the worst of it was actually having the physical experience.

There were many things on my mind at this time. First off, at this point I was only dating Wayne and not officially involved in a relationship. Secondly, this is the young man who really only wanted to buy me things and hang out with me and at times have sex. Would he now choose to become a permanent fixture in my life as the father of a child, even though we were not fully committed, engaged or even living together? It was not all the traditional circumstances I would have wished for, but these were the circumstances dished out to me and on my plate at this time. Once again I thought to myself, how could I let this happen? How could I for the third time, not protect myself in a situation that is highly protectable? At this point I had to eat what I was being served.

It was the winter of 1989 when I told Wayne I was pregnant and would be keeping the baby…no matter what. I didn't give him a choice in the matter to determine if he was interested in supporting my decision to keep this baby because my mind was already made up. If I had to go ahead and raise the child on my own as a single mother, I was prepared, at least mentally to do that. I would not put myself through the torment of taking the life of another one of my children. I had no intention of worrying about what he was going to say or not say to this new information I was going to share with him.

I had to tell Wayne over the phone that he was going to be a father since I was in Virginia and he was in NY. I told him that I took a pregnancy test and it was positive and then I sat quiet. I said yes, I am pregnant and intend to keep it. I shared with him at that point that I had already had two abortions and I had no intentions of having another one. There was silence for what felt like a whole day but after about five seconds he said to me, "Are you serious?" I said, "Yes, very serious," and he said, "Well, I guess we are having a baby then…"

Wayne was happy and I was completely shocked that he was happy to hear our news. This would be a life changing experience for both of us. He never gave me the feeling that it was not the right decision to make. He seemingly was prepared to go in this direction with me from the moment I told him. Although he didn't seem ready to propose marriage, I knew the time wasn't right to put that on the table. It seemed to me as if having a baby and getting married went together, like "Lisa & Wayne sitting in a tree, K-I-S-S-I-N-G, first comes love then comes marriage, then comes the baby in the baby carriage." Well it wasn't happening in that order this time. Although you think this is every girl's dream, I was not prepared for marriage at this point since the decision to have a baby was more than enough to handle. The decision to marry would require some more thinking to work through and possibly some difficult conversations so I left it alone.

We did in fact start to make plans to bring our lives together and every now and again talked about the possibility of getting married. He would always say, maybe next year. It was especially apparent that we had to figure out how to work together in this new, more formal relationship with a baby in the mix, but I was still only 19 years old. Now, the school year was ending and it was time for me to pack up and go back home. When I called my father and told him I was pregnant, he did not accept the thought as easily as Wayne had. He ultimately did not accept the news at all. After letting the facts sink in and truly hearing what I was saying, my father's response was that I was no longer welcome in his home and that I was not allowed to return there anytime soon, especially not while I was pregnant.

I was devastated at first since I did not know what I was going to do. I had the intention of going back home and carrying on my life in Uniondale where I grew up. This was the place I knew oh so well. Wayne had decided to move further south into North Carolina and re-start the business, which added to the complication of the whole situation. When I told my mother about my pregnancy she was definitely not surprised, however, she did sound as disappointed as I thought she would be. She definitely did not jump for joy, but she took it much better than my father. My mother was living with family and her husband JC at the time and there was obviously no room for me to consider living there. Nor did I think she would want to compromise her current living situation to bring on someone else, even though I am her daughter. It just was not an option for me to consider moving in with her then. At this time, Wayne suggested that I come and live with him in North Carolina and I agreed since I really had no other choice. I had no other idea where I would go. I appreciated him for stepping up and making the recommendation, which proved he was ready to raise our baby together with me.

I didn't have to put any of the stuff I had left behind in Virginia in storage because when I came back after returning from a visit to North Carolina to collect my things, most of it had been stolen. The landlord, who had long geri curls, acted like he had no idea what happened. I took what items were remaining which wasn't much and assumed he probably had something to do with the theft of my things. What remained were mainly clothes, but they had stolen my television, iron and a few other insignificant things.

Wayne and I found a small apartment in Durham, North Carolina in a house where we shared a room that had a very small kitchen and a bathroom. At the time, Wayne started to go to school again at North Carolina Central University which was within walking distance from our house just down the block. This was a similarly popular, large campus school like Virginia State University. As much as I also wanted to return to school, and knew I had to, attending a large university was not in the cards for me now for a few reasons. One, I was no longer getting my father's financial support to attend school and, secondly, I was afraid that if I considered attending another large university I would do the same thing I did at Virginia State; fail out and make a fool of myself. Eventually, I made the decision to go to the local Technical Community College in Durham, but that came much later. In the meantime, we played house and prepared for the arrival of our little baby. Wayne had saved a little money that he had from Virginia and his mother was also very financially supportive of him. When she found out I was going to have Wayne's baby she was very excited and overjoyed and not once ever made me feel like I had made the wrong decision. My mother and father, on the other hand, were very disappointed in me.

I did some research and found a local community doctor that I started going to for my regular pre-natal appointments. I did not have any healthcare benefits so I ended up applying for benefits on my own since I was now a single mother with no support. I was able to get approved for Medicaid and received as much support as I could to get myself prepared to do the scariest thing in my life I could ever have imagined. I attended my monthly pre-natal visits religiously and took my vitamins daily and did everything I was supposed to, on the doctor's orders.

By the time May 1989 came, I was about 5 months pregnant. Both my Mom and Dad were really upset with me. My mother continued to put me down when we talked on the phone. She was still regularly disappointed but couldn't get past the point that I had made up my mind and was moving ahead with my decision to have my baby. I had hoped she would just come to terms with my decision and support me on it. My Dad was so upset he wouldn't even talk to me at all. I prayed that one day he would understand the choice I made and eventually not be so disheartened with me.

Wayne and I talked about settling down together for real from time to time (not just living together) and again brought up the concept of us getting married. He responded by saying he doesn't want to get married before the baby was born. He thought he was too young. I reminded him that we talked about getting married possibly next year, but he began backtracking as if he didn't remember saying that at all. At this point it felt like I was being a little bit of an ass, as if I was the only one who wanted this togetherness, this family dream. It felt really fucked up to be the only one who wanted it. For some reason my heart was always tugging me in that direction, but I now know everything happens for a reason.

In these days Wayne and I spent so much time watching television. We watched soap opera stories all day starting with The Edge of Night, All My Children and One Life to Live and ending with General Hospital. It was a daily addiction for us. And what else can you do if you are pregnant and not working? Both Wayne and I were looking for a job, but nothing was coming through for either of us.

At one point Wayne left the house to go call his Dad. We had no house phone at the time. We had a regular habit of going to the phone booth to make all our phone calls. Since Wayne was on the run, we had to be careful how and who we talked to so the call could not be traced back to him. On this particular day, the house was a mess so I got up and decided to clean up. Our small studio apartment on Charlottesville Ave. in Durham was small, but it was cozy. Once I started cleaning I came across Wayne's wallet in a bag. When I looked in it, I saw three telephone numbers from who I assumed were some bitches he had met in passing. I was so pissed. I ripped them up and threw them away. When he came in, it seemed as if he knew I went through his wallet from how strange he was acting. When he found out, he got pissed and started cursing at me. He threw my purse outside which was so unnecessary as if to prove a point. What the hell was he doing with other girls' phone numbers?! I don't give a fuck who they were because, of course, he had an excuse about who they were. At that point I didn't even want to be in the house anymore. I ended up grabbing some money and walking down the street to the library. I found myself reading five chapters in a book before I was calm enough to go back home. When I got back home, the tension had passed and we moved on from this argument. There would be more.

We started to prepare for a trip to NY in early June of 1989. We had some trouble getting a car rental because of our lack of good credit. My brother Will came to meet us in Virgina and attempted to help us and couldn't get the car either. Will drove us to my sister's in Maryland and there we were finally able to get a car and headed to NY. I stayed with Tracey and Sam when we arrived in NY and went to visit my Mom a few times. She never knew the right thing to say to me. It was so awkward and, of course, she continued to look down on me with disappointment and resentment. Although I was a little more than 5 months pregnant at the time, I wasn't showing very much. I was very tiny with a little pouch for a belly. I was also still stick thin. Everyone in my family was pushing me to go see my Dad so I took the chance and tried to do that. Well, this ended up being a very bad idea. He kicked me out faster than I could get inside the door. He said, didn't I tell you not to come here!? From that moment on I knew it would be very difficult for my father to forgive me, but no matter what, I knew one day I would make him love me again.

We went back to North Carolina and on June 26th I went to the doctor's office for a regular monthly appointment. The doctor did his normal check of my blood pressure and the baby's heart rate and proceeded to do an internal exam of my uterus. I was six months pregnant with a due date of September, 1989. Wayne and I chose not to find out the sex of the baby in advance. Since it was our first time around we wanted to be surprised. In my mind I was absolutely positive it was a little boy. I felt that way based on the many myths you hear about pregnancy; I was carrying small and low and I felt generally good besides the morning sickness in the early weeks.

After completion of the doctor's internal exam, he had a very surprised and nervous look on his face. The doctor asked if I was having any pains and I told him possibly, since I had what felt like normal pregnancy back and crampy pain that I thought was typical for a pregnant person. He proceeded to tell me that based on what he found in the internal exam, it appeared as if I was already dilated by 2 centimeters. He was worried that my labor process had started. Whaaaat?! I did not know at first what he was talking about, but immediately following this conversation I was rushed into an emergency ambulance service and sent to Duke University Hospital. I didn't even have a chance to think any further about what I was feeling.

The doctor's office called Wayne and informed him of the update and he met me at the hospital. Upon arriving at the hospital I was checked again and told that I would have to be put on a regiment of medications in order to hold back the delivery of my baby or else he or she would be born quite prematurely and possibly not survive. At the same time I was told that I was also told that I would have to be on bed rest for the remaining length of my pregnancy, however long it would last, because at this point there was no telling when the delivery could happen. In order to ensure that I would not pose any further risk of the baby being born early, I would be laid up in the bed, not even able to leave it to use the bathroom. My natural activity and movement could pose a risk to the baby and make it come too early. At this point I was exactly 27 weeks pregnant. A normal pregnancy going full term would go from 38-40 weeks. I had more than 10 weeks to go.

The doctor told me that due to my experience of having two aborted pregnancies prior to this one my womb was making an assumption that this baby was going to be extracted sooner than its term just as the others had been. Hearing that news, I was devastated. I had believed I was going to have a baby based on my smart and ethical decision to keep it, and now I could possibly lose the baby because of my previous decisions to abort pregnancies. This was not making a whole lot of sense to me. Here, in fact, was where I was hit with a serious truth that the decisions you make in life can come back to haunt you and have an effect on future outcomes in your life. This is why it is very important to be thoughtful in every decision you make.

Well, I did everything I was supposed to and stayed in my hospital bed every day for the next month. Wayne came to visit me every day to bring me food and try to keep me encouraged. I was a bit depressed and worried that this pregnancy would end in horror once again. I prayed every day and hoped that God would spare me any devastation because I really wanted this baby and I really wanted to become a Mom, this time. I also wanted forgiveness for the previous decisions I had made to abort two babies. It was lonely in the hospital, and it was ironic that I had to stay here to save this pregnancy just as I had to stay overnight in the hospital to end my other two pregnancies. The difference was that this time I had to stay for many nights. No one in my family came to visit me. I just wanted this current nightmare to end.

On July 26th 1989, that day finally came. I awoke in the hospital that morning around 7 am as I had for a month, but that morning was different. At one point I felt a rush of what felt like urine or liquid pour out of my body uncontrollably. It felt like I was urinating on myself but I wasn't using the bathroom. I contacted the nurse to tell her about this unusual feeling. She tested the fluid and advised me that this was amniotic fluid and that the time had come for me to begin the labor process. I was immediately overwhelmed with fear, extremely excited, nervous and ready all at the same time. The doctor came in to do an internal exam and I was already 6 centimeters dilated. That means that the process of labor was moving forward and very quickly at that.

I was prepped and eventually moved into the labor and delivery room. I started to feel the pain of contractions coming on stronger and stronger in the two hours before the actual delivery. The contraction came every few minutes or so and it felt like the worst menstrual cramps you could ever get! It was like a pain pimple going up a roller coaster and as it went up the hill it got bigger and more painful and then the pain peaked at the top of the hill, as the roller coaster sped downhill, the pain released and then went away only to come back again the same exact way. Luckily it did not last a very long time and eventually the major contractions came closer together, faster, and faster and then it was time.

When it was time for me to actually push the baby out on the doctor's orders, it happened very quickly, and since the baby was still super tiny, that part was not very painful. It was actually a relief to have the last push come and to receive such a big blessing. The moment had arrived where I gave birth to my baby. To my complete and utter surprise, it was a GIRL! On Friday, July 26th at 10:39 am my baby girl was born! What an incredible feeling. They whisked her away very quickly and advised me of her weight, 3lbs and 6oz. She was immediately cleaned up and put into an incubator under yellow lights to ensure that her kidneys and other body parts were functioning properly based on her tiny little size and underdeveloped organs.

I am not sure why I had a feeling the baby would be a boy. I'd even picked out a name for him…his name would have been "Javon". I found it in the Bible. Javon appears in the Book of Genesis as the grandson of Noah. He was the son of Noah's son Japheth, from whom all Greek people are purportedly descended. The Hebrew Javan (Yavan) was used in reference to Greek people in general. Instead, when I met my new little baby girl I added an "A" to the end of her name and called her **Javona**. She was named **Javona Lisa Overton (JV)**. I gave her my first name as her middle name for a variety of reasons. I wanted her to be like me when she grew up. Also, my close friends and I had committed to naming our girl babies with our own middle name as a symbol of them being a product of us. Not long after, Riley had a girl and honored the commitment by naming her daughter Chantel Riley. Stella had a baby girl and named her Paige Stella. Sam had a baby girl and named her Elizabeth Sam and, just like that we started a trend among our circle of young mothers.

JV was in an incubator since birth due to how little she was. There were so many other little babies in the neonatal unit, some as small as one pound! Our JV was one of the biggest babies. This made me feel very happy as if I had better luck than any other mother who was worried about their premature newborn baby. Their baby who no one knew would even survive. Day by day it could be touch and go for any one of them based on their conditions. Some had jaundice, some had under developed lungs and/or hearts. My baby girl had everything...she was just very little and perfect.

I was released from the hospital a few days after JV was born. Wayne and I visited her in the hospital every day. About three weeks after she was born, we went to visit her and were very surprised to see my baby girl in an open bed! No more incubators. Wayne and I were shocked. All the nurses who worked that night gave us a round of applause as we entered the room and saw here there. We were so happy to see her thriving. Right before I had JV, I had started working at the Blockbuster Video store near our complex so I would leave the hospital in time to get to work by 6pm. I started to prepare to bring her home. I had to call the hospital about their Gentle Hug program. This was a program for the underserved, those mothers who didn't have much money. This allowed me to get a car seat for her as a rental for $20 for one year. I was supposed to go and reserve it, but I did not have the $20 to reserve the seat so I had to wait until the following week to make it up from work, all in preparation to get JV to come home. She had been drinking the breast milk I'd been pumping all along, but this day was the chance to breastfeed her for the first time, and I was so excited! The date was August 19, 1989. She did a couple of sucks off each breast, but that was all. I can't say that this was something I was really interested in continuing. I am not sure if that is a bad thing, but it felt very painful and it was a commitment I was not sure I could handle every day especially when I had to go to work. I just excited to do something that ultimately was supposed to be motherly, even though I had no idea what it was like to be a mother.

All in all, JV stayed in the hospital for a full month after she was born to take time to gain weight. Typically, in those days, they would not let you take the baby home until they were approximately 5 lbs. and thriving, drinking and sucking well and out of the (dark). JV was released from the hospital on August 26th. And to think she was not supposed to even make her way into the world until September. I was truly thankful to God for giving me another chance to experience pregnancy and bring life into the world. I was not going to take this for granted.

My mother and Wayne's mom came to see me shortly after she came home. I decorated JV's room like a real brand new baby girl's room with the help of Wayne's Mom, Grandma Gemma. She was so good to us. She sent us baby furniture; a crib and even a rocking chair that JV loved to fall asleep in when you were holding her. I rocked her to sleep there all the time. While I was getting adjusted to being a mother, I was still running up and down at times with Wayne. We went back and forth from Durham to Petersburg for him to collect work. We would take overnight trips to NY, literally drive there, meet his connection uptown in Harlem or wherever and turn right back around and go back down south to get the work on the street. At this time, Dominic, one of Wayne's team members, got arrested. This is a dude that lived around my way for my whole life. He was one year younger than me. Dominic came to college with us and then ended up getting caught up with Wayne and his boys. I almost felt guilty about this even though I didn't have anything to do with it, but I was sorry that he ever met Wayne and got into trouble. When the arrest happened, I started to be even more scared than I already was about the game Wayne was in. I knew I did not want him to be a part of it much longer, knowing we had a baby now. My goal was to try to get him out of it.

At this point Wayne had a few run-ins with the law. He and I got into an argument one night over a car rental and whose responsibility it was to take care of it and the argument got way out of hand. I called him ignorant, he called me a bitch and that was it. We were cursing at each other the whole way to the rental car place. When we got there he made me get out of the car and he pinned me down on the car, practically choking me. I yelled at him to stop but it was not in time. Out of nowhere these two men standing behind us grabbed him (and me because I had a hold of him) and threw us against the car. They were both holding Wayne's hands and practically breaking his arms. I started screaming at them to let him go. Eventually it was clear that they were police officers, detectives who just happened to be in the right place at the right time I guess for my sake. They took him downtown to the station. He was there on a $300 bond for assault of a police officer -- I guess for resisting arrest. He never had a chance to assault them. On top of all that, the way they handled me and treated me was uncalled for. I was supposedly the victim. I was so angry. I paid the bond to release him and we finished what we started, rented the car and headed to Petersburg.

On another occasion, Wayne and I were on our way to North Carolina. Wayne had asked me to drive and then he said forget it. I said let me drive! But no, he wouldn't. He was speeding like crazy and I was getting really scared. I told him to either slow down or let me drive and he just wouldn't. Before we knew it, the police were on his tail. Wayne was arrested that night for reckless driving at a speed of 105 mph. He had to pay a $200 fine and got a court date. I cried. I was so angry. We didn't talk the rest of the ride home. I was so tired of always being in a predicament with him.

After a while it was taking a toll on me. I had started smoking weed again. I stopped only briefly when I was pregnant, but barely. My job at Blockbuster Video down the road from our apartment complex was annoying me. I was working late shifts from 6 pm – midnight or after. I was tired of sorting out videos, vacuuming and cleaning up the place while dealing with customers. This is where I had my first real encounters of dealing with a boss and conflict. I couldn't stand the job, but I knew I had to have my own income coming into the house to attempt to show there were more than just drugs going on out there.

We had moved to a new apartment complex as soon as I had JV. It was a nice 2 bedroom apartment on the 2nd floor of a walk up. The dining room and living room were huge, overlooking the balcony to the parking lot. It felt really good to know we had our own real place and not the little room we had on the other side of Durham.

With all of that said, the fighting between Wayne and I was still going on. I was always under the impression that Wayne was seeing other women. At some point Bailey, his friend from high school started calling him on and off. He continued to tell me this was just his friend. In the middle of that, he also ended up getting busted dating some chick in the dorms in college. This chick called my house and told me that Wayne was leaving her dorm right now and that they had just been together. I was devastated to here this, but not surprised since this had been his MO for a while. I was feeling so frustrated and indifferent since I was sick of these kinds of incidents happening with him. A few minutes later, Wayne and his friend pulled up to the parking lot of our apartment building and I could see them from the balcony. I yelled out to them that they should just go back to where they came from because his girl from the dorm just called me and told me where he was coming from. She obviously called me to stir up an argument at home, and it worked. He ended up making a screeching U-turn and going back to the dorm and from what I understand; he ended up threatening this girl he was with, and cursing her out for calling me and who knows what else. Although I knew it was wrong, I felt little remorse because she obviously knew that we were together.

I met some great friends in North Carolina and also had a connection with an old friend from Long Island who also lived in Durham. She was going to school at NCCU and often came over to help me with JV. If she didn't have class and I had to go to work, she would stay until Wayne came home. All in all, living together with Wayne and raising our daughter, did not make it the family that I hoped it would be. I was having second thoughts about the relationship, I was missing home, and I was feeling very torn with the life I was living. To top this all off, JV was scheduled to have surgery on her eyes because she had suffered with crossed eyes since she was born. I was very concerned about it, and the doctor suggested she have an operation to correct it. Wayne and I were both very nervous about it but we just went ahead with it. We knew in the long run it would be best, and it was. She was only nine months old at the time. Waiting for her to come out of surgery was one of the most challenging days of my life. We brought her to the facility for the surgery around 6 am. They prepped her and told us exactly what to expect. They would be working on both eyes so her recovery process would be important to stay on top of, which included putting drops in her eyes three times a day and keeping an eye on any swelling. She came out of surgery and when the attendant rolled her out into the room I started to cry. I was just so happy that she was okay and I was emotionally drained from getting up so early and waiting for her to come out of surgery. She was fully healed after a few weeks.

8

Back To Long Island

I went back and forth to New York from North Carolina a few times for my family to see and meet JV. It was harder for them seemingly to come to North Carolina all the time so I didn't mind going there. I really missed home. I missed my neighborhood, my regular routines like Saturday morning chores while listening to Caribbean music, windows open and fresh smells flowing through the house while putting on some rice and peas on the pot with coconut milk and thyme. I would season the curry chicken, which was one of the only dishes I knew how to cook well. I wouldn't stay at home at my father's house because he still was not speaking to me like he used to. We only had very little small talk. One time I came to visit and went to see him, attempting to stay with him for the weekend. When I arrived and came inside, he was in his lazy boy chair as usual. I said hello and went into the kitchen. Tubs, who used to work at my house cleaning up and cooking for Daddy (who I eventually found out was his girlfriend) took JV and immediately started playing with her. When I came back into the living room my Dad and I started talking about the upcoming weekend and my plan to stay there. It was obvious he was not ready to agree to that. He made it clear that he was still not comfortable with me staying there with JV, even though I only had a temporary short-term visit planned so I said okay no problem. I called Stella and told her and she immediately said I could come and stay with her at her old house in Uniondale which was not far away. She still lived with her mom. Her mom worked nights as a nurse so we hardly ever got in her way.

When I got back to North Carolina, Wayne and I continued to argue and fight about one thing or another. He was still in the game, running his business as if it was the only thing that mattered. He was travelling back and forth to NY on a regular basis, leaving me and JV home alone more often. I was constantly finding girl's phone numbers in his pants pockets lying around and each time I found one, I made a mental note of it. I was bubbling with anger, and becoming sick of it. There was one last incident where this all came to a boiling point. I was once again on campus at Central, passing through, and was approached by a girl named Amanda. She was a little lighter than me, with long hair in a ponytail, was much shorter than me with a lot of hips and a lot of mouth. She proceeded to tell me the details of her dating Wayne and that my relationship with him was not real. She proceeded to tell me that he was only with me because of JV. I said well, is that so? After that encounter, I finally gave up on trying to make something work that was no longer working.

The last straw of proof came one day when we were both in the apartment and I overheard him on the phone with Amanda, talking just a little too sweet and cozy for my comfort, so I questioned him about it and then had a fit. He had a bunch of guys in the house bottling up work, including one of his friends who later on eventually ended up on America's Most Wanted. I walked into the living room from the bedroom and saw all the activity going on and I completely lost it! I started screaming that all of you knew that Wayne was cheating on me all of this time and you all acted like nothing was going on. Practically living in my house, in and out, staying over, greeting me as if all was good and I was a fool, naïve with no knowledge of what was going on. At that point, I slammed down every picture of us on the side tables and broke all the glass framed picture into thousands of pieces and told them "fuck you all" and then stormed out of the house. Around the same time, my girlfriend who was there from Long Island was also going through a break up with her boyfriend. We both left our places and stayed with a girlfriend of ours for a week to get ourselves together and think of a plan to move forward in the midst of our hurt and pain.

At this time JV was about a year old and I had started going to Durham Tech. I met a really nice guy there named Diego. We had a few classes together. I complained to him about Wayne and he tried his best to help build me up so I didn't worry about my situation. We would go out for lunch together and sometimes stop at his place since he was not far from our school. Diego was Puerto Rican and very nice looking. He was a little taller than me, had dark wavy hair and an awesome sense of humor. He lived with his parents at his home, but had his own space in the bottom half of the house. He took me to drop JV at daycare when Wayne was not around to take her and, sure enough, we became very close friends. At some point, Wayne must have been following me around. After I left Diego's place one afternoon Wayne approached Diego and threatened him to leave me alone. Diego told Wayne that I said we weren't together (because at that point we weren't together) but Wayne didn't want to let it go. He was attempting to scare him away. I was impressed to know that Diego stood up to him and didn't let Wayne bully him. I had some good times with Diego. We built a really nice friendship and eventually a nice companionship. I knew I would eventually move back to NY so a long-term/long distance relationship with him was not in the cards, however, our friendship was still very special. Unfortunately, at that point, it was too late for a relationship with Wayne. He had proven to me that he didn't respect me or love me so I made the decision to give it up. JV was almost 2 years old. I had been with him for 3 years at this point and it time to call it quits. I had to find the strength to care about myself and not stay in a relationship where I didn't feel loved and respected.

Over the next three months I started to build my plan to move away from North Carolina and get back to my home town of Long Island. I was still staying at the apartment that Wayne and I shared together but in separate rooms and JV was growing quickly. I was finishing school in the summer of '92 at Durham Technical Community College and would be getting my Associates degree in Liberal Arts. When I told my Dad I was going to be getting my Associates degree, he had a change of heart and decided to let me move back home. I was so thrilled and couldn't wait for school to be over with so I could get back into the place I belonged...home.

When the day came for me to move back to Long Island, my best friends, Olivia and Kennedy, were supposed to come and meet me in North Carolina. They were going to ride back with Wayne from a trip he took up there. He took JV with him at the time to leave her with his Mom since I would be moving all my stuff. My plan was to pack up to head back up north for good with my friends helping but for whatever reason it did not work out for Olivia and Kennedy to come and meet me. At that point I was so done with Wayne and this country town of Durham and the disappointment that had come with it that I did not care. I said I was going to do whatever I had to do to get out of there.

I knocked on my next door neighbor's front door and asked him and a few other guys to help me pack up my U-Haul truck with all of my belongings. I rolled three joints and jumped in the truck at 5:00

pm and got on the road from Durham all the way to New York...by MYSELF! I pulled up in front of Tracey and Sam's shop on Nassau Road in Roosevelt at 2 am with the best feeling of accomplishment I had ever felt. First, because I made it home safely, and second, because I did it all by myself with no support. This was one of the most accomplished things I felt like I had done in my whole entire life. Maybe it's because I had something to look forward to because that Sunday night I was going to the Kid Capri boat ride with my girls, and my old dudes from around the way, Brian, Dinco and Trevor, also known as Charlie Brown, Dinco and Busta Rhymes; Leaders of the New School. That night I went out on the boat ride and had a damn good time and I truly celebrated my freedom from Wayne and North Carolina. My new focus was to re-build my relationship with my Dad, find a job, and get back into school immediately so I could work on getting my Bachelor's degree.

Once I settled into my old house and room with JV I was able to get a new job at American Express through Stella who was working there at the time. My mother was helping me out with JV. It was a customer service position answering calls for people ordering through the AMEX catalog. It was a decent job for what I had to do. I had no car, so I was taking the bus to Manhasset every day. It was difficult for me to get used to since I was accustomed to having my own car in North Carolina and whatever cash I needed through Wayne's support, so this was a huge transition. It was different to have to consistently work and make sure that I got there on my own. I started hanging out again with my old crew, Olivia, Kennedy, Tracey and Sam, and everything just started to fit right back into place for me.

I was still adjusting to living back at home with my Dad, especially since he had this woman Tubs living in the house with us. Tubs was a very big woman. She was tall, heavier set and broad, so visually she was quite intimidating looking because she was huge, Amazon-like. When she spoke, she had a very timid little tiny voice which did not fit her look. I think it was her way of trying to seem pretty. She was not very attractive at all to me and I never understood why my Dad had her living there. I just kept telling myself that she was the maid. At one point I was on the phone with Olivia and Tubs picked up the phone twice, and on the second time said she said she wanted to make an important call. I said okay, fine. When I hung up the phone I went and asked her what her problem was with me. I tried to speak as calmly as I could to this big bitch. I then left her room and made my way over to my Dad who was in the living room at the time. Then this bitch came downstairs talking shit. She says all I can do is bring home a baby to my father! What? She should have never said that. I said oh, now I see what is going on. You are jealous! I knew that was her problem the whole time. She was 36 or older and had no children. My father said not to say anything and I said what little I could then I stormed out of the house. When I came back the argument continued. She was bragging to me about what she has including her

4-bedroom house in Jamaica, her car, her money and saying how she is better off than me. I said you better be better off than me. You are damn near 40 years old! I said you have no life, no friends, no kids and no love!

At that point she and I had a personal vengeance against each other. Back then I wished that bitch never came into my life. That goes as far back to say that I wish my mother never left because that's why that bitch came into the house. I couldn't wait for her to move her ass out. Complaining that I don't take care of my Dad when how could I? She sweated him constantly, waiting on him hand and foot. Who does she think took care of him when her fat ass wasn't here? When my mother left home, I was there. I washed all the clothes, made dinner for Daddy and my brothers, went to church with my Dad every Sunday, cleaned the house every week…I did everything inside the house. The boys and Daddy did everything outside the house. Tubs was an immature, no life having, fat, introverted, anti-social, ugly, and jealous bitch! She was always acting weird. I thought she needed a psychiatrist. In the end, about 2 years later, her and my father had a falling out. She was so angry about their separation that she took my father to court for money she thought she had contributed to their relationship. By that time, he had moved to Florida. The judge honored her claim of $5000. Less than a year later, she died of a heart attack. End of story.

My 22nd birthday was coming up. Olivia and I were born in the same month, eight days apart. We made plans to go hang out at the club Spectrum in East Meadow to celebrate, but it was closed that night for a private party and you had to be 23 to get in…that was such a bummer. We were so ready. That night we met up with Spencer and Rick. I hadn't seen Spencer in almost a year. He knew I had JV and I knew he had a daughter named Sydney also. We ended up in the parking lot across from Eisenhower Park and smoked a joint outside the Cigar store on Hempstead Tpke. Olivia and I ended up riding with the guys to Queens to get more weed and then we parked up to roll up some more. It was a while since I had seen Spencer and, at one point, everyone slowly stepped away so he and I started to talk.

We talked about old memories and the good times we had on Manor Pkwy. We talked about our first kiss and when he rode his bike over to my block. It was the night my sister was christening her son and I snuck away from the house to meet him, and since everyone was all caught up in the party no one even noticed I was gone and I was only 13. I had broken up with Wayne so it had been seven months since I'd had sex with him and two months since I'd been with Diego. I wanted to kiss Spencer so bad and tell him how much I still loved him, but with the others around it felt awkward. When Spencer was around me it made me feel just like I did when we first met. I had butterflies in my stomach, shaky nerves and a huge lump in my throat.

In essence we just laughed and talked until the crew came back over and we promised each other that we would stay in touch.

I got my first car on the road two days before my 22nd birthday. It was a Pulsar that used to belong to my cousin, then my brother Tony, then me! I drove it to work for the first time on my birthday. When I got off the highway at exit 33 on the Northern State Parkway it broke down on me on my way to work. Go figure. I had to walk the rest of the way to work in the pouring rain. My birthday always brings very exciting and unusual things to the table! When I got to work, Stella and some other friends that I work with decorated my cubicle with balloons, cards and gifts. All and all, it ended up being a nice day. With all of that said, I was very happy to be back home.

Later that day I received a phone call from Sam that brought to life one of my biggest fears. The fear I always had from the days I tried to stay away from Wayne all the way up until the day we broke up. The bad news she shared was that Wayne had been arrested in North Carolina and locked up. This was the news I always knew would one day come. Ultimately, he was charged with weapons conspiracy. Another partner he was working with at the time was also charged with drug trafficking. It was something that I feared for a while. Even though we were no longer together, I had become more afraid for him. Three years before this, Mackenzie and Leo had been arrested for the same thing. His time had come. I prayed for him and asked God to protect him during what would be a trying time for him and Grandma Gemma and I hoped that everything worked out for the best.

I did eventually go down south with his Mom to attend a court date when he was about to get sentenced. After the sentencing, I met with his attorney and he told me Wayne would be out of JV's life for a short time until she was of age to be running around and going to school. At that time she was 2. Ultimately, with a plea deal and a reduced sentence, he would be home in about three years. At this point our relationship was already over, but with that news, it officially came to an end.

When I transitioned back to Long Island, I continued getting back on my feet. Daddy had started to make plans to move down to Florida. He had retired from the construction business shortly after I came home and was getting prepared to put the house on Myron Street on the market for sale. My brother Will and I decided to get an apartment together and we started looking around in Queens since everything in Long Island was so expensive. We eventually did find a cute little house in Queens Village. Will had the first floor and I took the loft upstairs where JV and I had our own little special space. It was great to be in my own place, even though it was with Will. I never really wanted to live alone, so it was comforting to know we were together. It was unusual being a single mother and I felt pretty lonely, but I was focused on getting my life in NY back together. I had received my Associate's degree and was ready to work on getting my Bachelor's degree.

I ended up leaving my part-time job at American Express shortly thereafter and got a full-time job at JFK Airport at an airline called Tower Air. It was convenient for me since I now lived in Queens and it was a short ride to the airport from my house. I was a Reservations Agent. Basically, when customers called to book flights to the places where Tower Air flew, I made their reservation through the system. The airline was an Israeli company. I had never heard of them before I applied and was happy to get the opportunity to start working there. I guess I hadn't heard of them since I had no intention of traveling to Israel anytime soon. I had a full-time schedule and felt so mature going to work. This was where I gained a great understanding of what it was like to work full-time and provide customer service to people.

My hours were 8-4. There were about 15 of us in a room with a line of computers and headsets on. Most of us were young adults trying to make ends meet. My boss John was the supervisor and his wife also used to work with us. John was big and brolick with blonde hair and she was tiny and petite with short, dark hair. She reminded me of Janet from Three's Company. One of my friends that I met there, Kitty Vega, had worked there for a while and everyone loved her. She was a little older and this company was something she truly made a career out of. At this point I was not thinking that far ahead in my life to know that this would be a career choice or not, but she was definitely very serious about her work. She'd come to work on the weekends to get extra hours, and she played a different role then. She was one of the crew at the ticketing gate that checked people in for their flights. I went to work with her one day because I was curious to see how it worked and I wanted to get some overtime hours. I had to be there by 4:30 am which is the time that passengers arrived for early flights. It was definitely hard work. She would mostly work the flights that were going to Israel and to San Juan, Puerto Rico. Eventually, Tower Air started to fly to Sao Paolo, Brazil. From way back then I always wanted to go to Brazil, but I couldn't picture myself actually doing it. One reason is because it was pretty expensive. The other reason is that I developed a massive fear of flying.

When I took the job at the airport I was hesitant to take it because of my fear, but then I said it's not like I am becoming a flight attendant, so I am not being forced to go anywhere or travel frequently. I am just at the airport with millions of planes flying over my head every day. Eventually, I did get the desire to travel. I also had great travel benefits. My Mom used them more than I did because she liked to travel back and forth to Florida to visit family members and she was able to use my benefits to fly for free. She was comfortable with flying on standby and always got through to get a seat at the airport.

One day I decided to gear up and take a trip. Stella and I made plans to go see Tracey and Sam in Florida because by that time, they had moved down to Ft. Lauderdale to start a business. They eventually opened two hair salons that they called Setting Trends Naturally. It was a natural hair salon. They focused on promoting hair care that was natural and not using methods like perms and relaxers aka the creamy crack to style your hair. Stella and I made our plans together and we even brought along one of my co-workers who worked at the airline with me. Her name was Eliza.

We were all super excited for the trip and got packed up and ready to go. Eliza brought her little son and I brought JV. They were both four at the time. They had a great time playing together before getting on board the big 747. I was super nervous to fly, but handled it very well on the flight to Ft. Lauderdale. My friend Eliza though, didn't handle it that well at all. She panicked and was very upset by the flight and decided that she did not want to stay the weekend as we had planned and went back to the airport the next day and went back to NY. Stella and I stayed for the rest of the weekend, and spent time with Tracey, Sam, Aunt Joy and Sam's kids and had a great time catching up on good old times.

We went back to the airport on Sunday, boarded the flight back home and midway through, my biggest fear came to life. The flight was caught in a horrendous lightning storm. The pilot got on the loud speaker and told everyone that we were flying through a very bad storm and he did not have enough time to divert it. He directed the flight attendants to their seat and as he did that, the plane dropped dramatically and subsequently roller coaster dipped and turned through the storm. You could very clearly see the lightning striking through the windows because it was dark out. The flight attendants were thrown down the aisle, bumping into chairs as they struggled to get to their seats. The look of panic on their faces was something I will never forget. The turbulence was unbelievable. I panicked and made sure my seatbelt was buckled. I closed my eyes and said a short prayer and held onto JV very tightly. She wasn't fully aware of the experience we were going through and had no idea of the dread that was creeping into my body thinking that the plane was going to crash at any moment. All the while this was happening Stella slept through the whole entire thing! She was good for that. She could sleep on top of a pumping speaker at a club which she did from time to time when we went out. The plane did eventually land safely at JFK airport. I was so traumatized that I vowed to never fly again. Something I learned much later on in life is "never say never"…

9

My First Love Returns

My brother Will and I had been enjoying our time in our little home in Queens. We had been living together for about a year before we had a huge falling out. He was supposed to pay our water bill, and didn't, so one day after coming home from work I found out we had no water in the house. This is the worst feeling when you are looking forward to coming home to a hot shower. This wasn't the first time something like this had happened. On another occasion he took a little car I had bought and borrowed it to drive to Albany to visit his girlfriend at the time. The car broke down on him at some point on the road and he left it there without contacting me or attempting to get it back. At the end of the day, we ended up going our separate ways. He moved to the Bronx and I moved on and started re-connecting with my first love, Spencer. Spencer and I had always remained in touch via phone after I went away to college. We talked from time to time or I would see him on Manor Pkwy when I came home from school briefly on the block or over at Tracey and Sam's when we were hanging out in the neighborhood.

When I officially made the decision to leave North Carolina after Wayne cheated on me a few times, I looked forward to being home in Long Island. Interestingly enough, when I was making plans to come back home, Spencer was also having trouble with his relationship with his girlfriend at the time named Diana. Diana was the mother of his two children, Sydney and Samuel. By the time I came back to Long Island Sydney was 5 and Diana was pregnant with Samuel. Diana and Spencer were in the same grade in high school where they met. She was brown-skinned, about 5'4", and had really long straight hair, a very nice looking girl. She was also a twin. She lived on the other side of town and once I went away to college, Diana and Spencer's relationship grew into something more. They lived together in an apartment on Long Island and attempted to start a life together. However, once Spencer and Diana broke up, he made a decision to move out of the apartment they had together and move back home with his mom for a short time. At that point, he and I started to engage more seriously about rekindling our relationship. We started officially dating again (after a six year break up since high school) and eventually I ended up moving into his mom's house in Roosevelt. By then Diana had moved back home with her mother in Queens.

At first I thought this was going to be a great big happy family situation since I am always so optimistic about everything. However, there was a lot more turmoil than I expected. First of all, Diana was not very happy about the fact that she and Spencer broke up when she was pregnant with Samuel, and rightly so. Secondly, it was obvious that since we moved into his mother's house, it would be certain that we would run into each other there. Thirdly, the fact that Spencer's mother and three sisters were now in the middle of all the details did not make the situation any better. At times they found it difficult to remain neutral and most times chose Diana's side in the arguments, which was disruptive. I got the impression that they were afraid that Diana would keep them away from the children, which is exactly what seemed to happen at times.

His mother argued all the time about leaving things on the stove in the kitchen, she would complain about how I was raising my JV, and you name it, there was always an argument about something. She pretty much had an attitude with me about most things. My impression is that Spencer's mom was not happy with Spencer being around my daughter JV when he was not living around his own kids and I felt as if she thought JV didn't deserve to have a father-like experience with him. I never felt like she was on my side, but I kept my mouth shut. I felt like I had to continue to protect JV from what I was feeling. Once or twice in conversation I complained about things Spencer did or said and that turned out to be a really bad idea because they used it against me later on. When Spencer and I argued they, of course, took his side, telling him things I may have said out of context and leaving me feeling like an outsider. After the last argument in the house I just could not take it anymore and I wasn't mature or savy enough to have kept my feelings to myself. I told my father that it had become difficult getting along in the house with Spencer's family and since my old house was still up for sale and there were no offers on it yet, he gave the okay for me and Spencer to stay there – 1114 Myron St. I am going back home.

When my Dad heard that I was having a hard time getting along with Spencer's mother and his sisters, I really think he felt sorry for me and found a place in his heart to help me. I had hoped that maybe he was feeling remorseful about not talking to me when I got pregnant with JV. Spencer's family always chose Diana's side of arguments and I felt like I was putting myself in an unrealistic and losing situation. I had my own family and I had to take a moment to lean on them to figure out how to get my life back together. I was so happy when Daddy gave me and Spencer the okay to move into my old house. We jumped on it quickly. My brother Tony was already living there, and eventually his girlfriend at the time moved in as well.

Diana and Spencer made arrangements about how and when he would come to pick up Sydney. The first time we ran into each other I was in the car with him when we arrived at Diana's mother's house to pick Sydney up for the weekend. When Spencer went inside, she found out I was in the car and literally lost it. They started to argue inside the house and she ran around the house trying to get to the front door, apparently to come outside and approach me. Spencer and her mom held her back and made her stay inside and we never came into contact with each other. This was the beginning of a pretty rough battle. At the time Diana was pregnant so I can understand the pain and hatred she had for me.

The night of June 19th 1992, Diana gave birth when we were all at Kennedy's birthday celebration that Carter had arranged at the Hilton hotel in Queens. We were there with Rick, Doug and a bunch of other people. We got drunk and smoked a few blunts. John had this crazy dude named Gee with him. Gee is a real asshole. He was acting up like a jerk around JV the last time I met him and I did not like that shit at all. I had a brief argument with Spencer telling him that I didn't want him holding his drunk friends up all night long and Doug over heard me. He stepped out of nowhere like, yeah? Anyway, I stood my ground and spoke out about how I felt. I said you guys are always getting drunk and you need to learn how to handle it. When I got to my limit lately, I chilled, since I had to drive everyone home. No one else seemed to know their limit. Maybe having JV now opened my eyes to this a little more. I can't be running around drunk with a little child in tow.

When Spencer and I got home that night, we made love. We made crazy promises to each other. I told him that if he fucked anyone else he would never see me again. I would expect him to do the same. I said I was ready to commit myself to him 100% so if that is the case, it has to go both ways. I was adamant about not getting caught up in the same situation I was in with Wayne. Spencer always told me how much he loved me and wanted to marry me, etc. so I was just hoping and waiting for that precious day to come.

The next morning was Saturday. I jumped up at 8:30 am to go to work. Spencer was complaining of a headache and that he was not going to work so he sent me to work with his car. At 12:30 Spencer's sister beeped me. When I called her back she told me that Diana had a baby boy yesterday named Samuel. My face dropped. In a way, it was a relief that she had a healthy baby, but then a feeling of depression set in. What next? I called Spencer right away and he was already on the phone with Diana. He told me he was very happy, but also angry because she hadn't called him earlier at the time to tell him about the birth of his son. He knew she wouldn't call right away so he shouldn't have been angry. His friend, Dutch, took him to the hospital to see Diana and Samuel. Ironically, on Father's Day, Spencer brought the car seat to the hospital to pick up Diana and Samuel and bring them home. For the next several weeks, all the talk was about Diana and Spencer's baby. I felt kind of jealous knowing he wasn't our baby; he was theirs, which I think was a natural reaction to have. After aborting our baby, once again I felt very sad and betrayed.

At that time Spencer and I were talking about marriage, I ended up getting pregnant not long after Diana had Samuel, before any real thoughts about a wedding were in place. I was finally going to have Spencer's baby and I was very excited about it. Not long after that, I couldn't hold back and I formally proposed to him. He and I were in the house just relaxing and watching television and I told him that we would spend the rest of our lives together so we might as well just get married. He didn't say no, but he didn't absolutely say yes either. Spencer was my first love and I always knew we would be better together and that we would find each other's love again. In my heart I knew he was my soul mate. I am not sure that Spencer would have taken the step to propose if I didn't put it out there to him. I always wonder what would have happened if I did not propose to him. Eventually he did agree that it was our plan to be together and he confirmed that yes, he would marry me.

At the time, I was getting a lot of pressure from my mom to get married before the baby was born. I am sure she felt embarrassed that I was having another baby and was not married yet. With this pressure on my back I tried to talk Spencer into getting married before I gave birth since I was due in January of 1994 but he refused to do it. Instead, I conceded that he was right, that we should follow through on our original plans and I stopped pressuring him and we kept our original wedding date of May 14th, 1994.

I wrote my Dad a letter to ask him if it was okay to have the wedding in the backyard at our house on Myron St. since we didn't really have a lot of money to afford booking a nice hall. My graduation date was on May 22nd so it would be a very busy month. I was attending Old Westbury working on my Bachelor's degree in Sociology while I was pregnant and I couldn't wait to be finished.

Getting my degree was close to the finish line and I was due to have the baby soon. I was working full-time, going to school full-time and planning a wedding while I was pregnant, and doing all this literally by myself, but I was happy to be conquering all of my desired goals and wishes. I stuck to the plan, no matter how difficult it felt at times. It was frustrating, I cried often, but I knew it would all get better one day.

One morning Spencer and I took Samuel to the hospital for X-rays because he was always getting ear infections. He was scheduled to go into the hospital for an operation to put tubes in his ears the next day. Spencer was really worried and I don't blame him. I encouraged him to go with Diana to the surgery. She had said her boyfriend at the time was also going and at first Spencer didn't want to go and be put in the situation of being around her boyfriend, but then he changed his mind and said he didn't care. It's his son and he should be there.

He let anger get in the way at first. I am sure it must have been awkward, but it is something they would have to get used to. I wish I could have gone also, but I had JV with me. Spencer and I talked about my feelings if/when he went and he didn't want me to get mad. I was not mad at all, but he said he still wouldn't want Wayne to come anywhere with me. Unfortunately, these situations are to be expected when relationships split up and there are children involved. Our insecurities have to take a back seat to what's best for the kids. I predicted there would be many more occasions, events and moments when we would all have to be in the same room and we needed to prepare now to manage them.

The next Sunday I had my baby shower. It was a total surprise, but it was disappointing because hardly anyone showed up. The weather was not that great in January. There was a snow storm brewing at the same time and many were unable to make it because of the pending snow. My mother wasn't even coming because she was not feeling well and didn't even call anyone to say so. I am not sure why she didn't even call me or my friends to say something. Once again I assumed that she was disappointed I was pregnant again and not married. I couldn't seem to find any way to get her to be happy with me. It was heartbreaking. Of course, a few of my close friends were there. I cried at first for the surprise. I wanted people from work to come also, but it just was not possible. None of my family was there. In the end, it was a cozy gathering of my closest friends, Olivia, Stella and Kennedy, even Riley was there from Harlem and my girls from Brooklyn. I was thankful for them.

About eighteen months after Samuel was born, our little girl was born on January 31st 1994. It all started that Sunday when I decided to bring Spencer to church with me where we would be married in a few short months. In the middle of the service I started to get contractions every 10 minutes or so. It lasted for the entire day until around 5:00 pm. Then they started to come even faster, about every six minutes. That's when I called the doctor. I gave him all my information, how often the contractions were coming, how I was feeling and he advised me to come into the hospital.

I arrived at Franklin General Hospital ironically, where I had received confirmation of my first pregnancy that was aborted. Of all the people to be my doctor that evening, it was a doctor who had given my mother the results of my pregnancy test back in high school. I had no choice but to see him. When the doctor did the initial exam he was in the middle of watching the super bowl game. The Dallas Cowboys were playing the Buffalo Bills. He barely looked at me while doing the exam because he was so caught up with the game. He didn't feel that I was ready and he left, saying he would be back later on when he did his rounds. When he came back later in the evening and performed another exam, they noticed that the baby was showing as a "face presentation". I was told that this was not a good sign. He informed me they had to do a caesarian section and I became immediately upset and started to cry. I was scared and upset because at that point I knew they would not allow Spencer to be present for the birth and I really wanted him there with me. I was also upset to know that I was going to be cut open and not have the baby naturally, which is what I had prepared for all along. They prepped me for the operation, brought in the anesthesiologist who put the mask over my face and once again asked me to count backwards from 10. My heart was racing and I felt lost, as if I was going to die.

Spencer held my hand and gave me a reassuring look as I was put under the anaesthesia. He was able to stick around up until they started opening me up. He told me that after they opened me up he could see them move all my organs to the side from outside the operating room. A little after midnight at 12:37 am our baby girl was born. I didn't fully recover until about 4am. Spencer was at my side telling me it was a baby girl weighing 7lbs, 4ozs. and I just kept saying, "It's a girl, it's a girl?" I was so delirious and out of it. I was pretty surprised it was a girl. Just like with JV for some reason, I thought they would both be boys. I was thrilled but surprised.

Spencer went home and came back later that evening and at that point made a decision that he wanted to name our baby girl Jazmin after Princess Jazmin from the movie Aladdin. We talked forever about what names we had in mind. If she was going to be a boy we considered Shane. The other girl name we liked was Mariah but we settled on Princess Jazmin Angelle and it fit her so well. I kept my theme of having my babies get my name also, so Princess received my middle name while JV had my first name as her middle name. I was in love with my girls.

Since I was recovering from a C-section, I had to stay in the hospital for a week. I received lots of visitors and didn't mind all of the attention at all. I attempted to breastfeed Princess for one week but it was hurting so bad I couldn't take it. My body was aching and when Princess grabbed onto my nipple I'd scream in pain. I stopped trying to breastfeed completely on Monday, and then Tuesday was the worst. My chest felt like it was full of bricks. My chest was hard and swollen! The lumps were so bad I it made me feel like what I thought having lumps from cancer might feel like. It was awful. I was taking Motrin all day and Spencer had to watch after Princess because I could not move without crying in pain.

The day I was scheduled to bring her home, there was no oil in the tank at the house and it was so cold. More snow had come. I was mad as hell at my brother Tony because that was his responsibility to buy oil and keep it in the tank so we could have heat. We split the bills in the house and he was supposed to make sure there was oil in the tank. I ended up having to stay at my Aunt's house for the day until the oil tank was up and running. My mom was also living with my Aunt at the time. I was so angry because I wanted to be home in my own house with my new baby.

When we got home and settled, I overheard Spencer and Tony talking. Eventually, his girlfriend barged into the conversation to have a word with Spencer also. At one point I started to hear her voice rise up and I went downstairs to see what was going on. It ended up that we got into a huge argument and she said a little more than was needed. She apparently was upset because my father wanted me to have a key to the back door which was the entrance to their part of the house and she didn't like that fact at all. I said if she didn't like it, then she could leave! She claims she didn't give a fuck about anybody in my family. I told her that nobody gave a shit about her either. She cursed me out with all kinds of names. Spencer was surprised that Tony was allowing her talk to me that way without correcting her. I realized Tony wouldn't take my side over hers and I immediately called Daddy and told him the situation and of course he wasn't too pleased. He told Tony to stop letting this girl dictate rules in our house. So at that point she started storming around and moving her stuff the hell out. I didn't know if Tony was leaving with her or not. I really don't know what was on Tony's mind in that moment. Eventually he did decide to move out. We didn't talk for a while after that argument. My father said it was okay to get someone else to rent out the basement when they moved out so I told Stella she could move in since she was also looking for a place at the same time. She was so happy to move in with us and I was too.

Spencer and I had been living with Princess for about two weeks when he came home and surprised me with an engagement ring on Valentine's Day, Feb. 14, 1994. When he arrived at home that night from work, he pulled me to the side and showed me the box. I had an idea what it was. He opened it and told me he loved me and that he wanted to give me the ring for a while but he couldn't afford to, so he paid down on it over the past six months with half of his check each week. At that point I started to cry because he was so sweet and I knew that it wasn't easy for us financially at that time. This was one of the most important moments in my life. I felt so loved by him and special in that moment.

When I gave birth to Princess it was over the winter break from college. I went right back to school when the semester started again. I had to go to class after getting my ring and I could hardly think with my new ring on my finger. It wasn't a huge diamond, but it was my diamond. I was so happy. We had the official engagement party at the end of February 1994, 3 months before our wedding. We were planning to have it at the house. Spencer and I would cook and everyone offered to bring something. Spencer had been working in restaurants since he was in high school so he was a great cook.

I called my Dad and gave him all the details about the engagement party. He wasn't planning to attend since he was in Florida, but I just wanted him to know what was going on in his house since we were expecting a lot of people to attend. That night I got home from school at 8 pm. My mom was helping with the girls so she stayed at the house when I was at school. It was some minutes after 10 this night when I was writing in my diary about planning for the party and the girls were both fast asleep. I peeked in on them at one point and just paused in awe of the fact that we were growing our family and seriously beginning to bring our lives together. I continued making calls about planning our engagement party since the day was quickly approaching.

So many people showed up for the part. It was pretty casual. We played games and had a lot of fun. Princess refused to go to sleep that night. She was up until 1 am. Just a little nigh owl. I didn't spend that much time enjoying the party because I wanted to keep her away from the living room where everyone was visiting. She was still a very newborn baby. Eventually, she did fall asleep.

At one point during the party, we watched the "Old School" video I had from Tracey and Sam's basement. This was a series of episodes of us kids in the basement of Tracey, Sam and Rob's house when we were younger. We danced and partied in front of the video and saved the recordings of the antics. We also played the game Scattergories. I was excited about what was coming up in the next three months; our big day. When we got in bed that night Spencer told me he wanted to make love. I was hesitant since I was only three weeks postpartum, but I wanted him just as bad. We had a quick moment of love making and he pulled out before it could become a problem (fingers crossed) and of course I was immediately concerned because I DO NOT want to get pregnant again, at least not now.

Sometimes a moment of passion can lead to life long decisions that you can't turn back from. I know this from experience.

Not long after having Princess we got up and went over to Spencer's mom's house to bring Princess for a visit. When we got there, Diana was in the living room. She said hi to me and I said hi back. I brought Princess into his sister's room and his sister June rushed up behind me to see her. She took her out and brought her over to her other sister, Josie, who was confined to the bed. One thing I knew for sure about Spencer's family is that they loved babies. They awed over her and passed her around. Diana walked in and out at one point. I assumed she wanted to get a glance of Princess. I don't blame her since if she were me; I would have also wanted to see her. I am sure she saw her better after we left. For once, I was happy to know that they had an interest in my daughter, even if they didn't have a real interest in me.

The next day there was a huge snowstorm. There was so much snow that it was a disaster. It had to be at least ten feet. Spencer had been running around all day. He didn't have to go to the restaurant because of the snow, yet he was still at home working around the house. He had a carpet cleaner he used and then he returned and shoveled snow at our place and at his Mom's house. He went with John to Brooklyn, cleaned the carpet in Roosevelt also, and then cooked dinner. When he was just about to relax, his mother called saying she was stuck at her job due to the snow so Spencer had to go and get her. He was pissed because he was visibly stressed and tired and he stormed out of the house screaming, saying he was sick of this shit! Before he left, he punched a hole in the wall. I tried to stop him on his way out but he warned me not to say a word. I immediately became worried that I was about to get involved in a very volatile situation, both with getting in-between Spencer and his family, and dealing with his temper. I worried what I was getting myself into if this continued after we got married.

We had a ton of bills and he was also contributing to his family's household expenses so again, I wondered if I should be worried. I wasn't sure how I was supposed to handle this. I wouldn't say much of anything which is something I was good at. I had a tendency to keep my feelings inside and act as if everything was okay when it really wasn't. I can relate to his need to support his mom and accepted that this was how it would be. I recalled stories I had heard of my Dad having to support his mom back in the day. My father worked very hard to build a house for his mother back in Jamaica when she helped to take care of his dozens of kids. I can only assume my mother may have also been feeling neglected while he contributed to his Mom's household and the other children he had to raise. At the time, I figured I needed to just concentrate on finishing school and finding another job so my own income would be secure. These times were difficult enough for us as it was, and I could only pray that everything would be okay.

Later that month I went back to work at Tower Air after my maternity leave. At this time I had been having this nervous, tense feeling in my heart for over a week. I kept thinking subconsciously about death and dying. I can only assume that I had been feeling this way because there was so much going on in my life. I was under a lot of stress with school, going back to work and also planning our wedding. Everyone tried to tell me that these feelings were normal and that people go through these things at different points in their lives. I wasn't so sure since it didn't feel normal to me so I went to the doctor and told her how I had been feeling; including physically dizzy, loss of appetite, tired, and literally depressed. She explained that I was going through something called postpartum depression. It feels like I had it in a severe form. I don't know why I was obsessed with death and worried about it so much since anyone could pass away at any time, but I was obsessed with thinking about it and putting myself in the position of being dead in my mind. I just wondered what came after this life, if there is anything. I believe in God and I know He will lead me through, but I was so busy that these negative thoughts took me all over the place.

I was super excited about the wedding and my upcoming graduation that I became overwhelmed with the thoughts of having it not all happen in time and that I would lose my life before all these great things happened for me. My fiancé loved me and I had two beautiful daughters…what else did I need? For some reason it just always felt like I didn't have enough and it's possible my feelings of depression were increasing those feelings of irrationality, fear and death.

During this time I had started smoking a hell of a lot of weed again so I kept trying to talk myself into not smoking as much. I was becoming aware that it was just too much. Stella and I went to a party after picking up fabric material for my bridesmaid dresses and I drank and smoked so much at the party. I was so sick, I thought I was dying and it was all over. I was praying that nothing happened to me that night. From that night on I said I wouldn't do that ever again. I was starting to come to grips with life and I began to realize that life is very important and you shouldn't waste precious time on artificial and abusive highs at an aggressive level. I ended up taking a blood test a few days later because I thought I was pregnant, but thank God the test was negative. By this time Stella had officially moved downstairs because Tony had moved out. I felt hurt by the whole thing. I really didn't feel like he took up for me in the argument with his girlfriend.

The date finally came for our wedding day. We had planned a small wedding in the backyard of our house, approximately 100 people, but in my opinion it was very nicely done. Although Spencer and I were both working, at the time we got married we were trying our best to manage our combined expenses and limit any excess spending on the day of the wedding. I was working at Tower Airlines and by this time I had been promoted to the Reservations Supervisor in their call center. I remember going on tour of one of the 747 planes that we flew. It was crazy to sit in the pilot's seat knowing that I was deathly afraid to fly. Spencer was working as a cook at the North Shore Steakhouse. I did all of the wedding preparation on my own, but Spencer managed the relationship with a local caterer we found in Hempstead, named Henry Smith Caterers, since that was his expertise. Spencer wanted to cater the whole thing himself but I told him that would be impossible since he would be too busy with his groomsmen and too stressed so he agreed to hire someone. I used Sandy's in East Meadow to prepare all of the decorations. They put up the tent three days before and prepared all the balloons and centerpieces the day of the wedding which were all very nicely done. The air was bursting with excitement.

The weather was perfect. It was in the low 70's, comfortable, sunny and breezy. Our colors were teal blue and white. His groomsmen wore black tuxedos with teal blue ties, and accessories. My girls wore teal blue dresses that were all handmade. My father walked me down the aisle. As he escorted me down the aisle, my father, the out-going and well-liked man that he was, shook hands with guests. He was beaming with pride. I could see by the look on his face that this was an important day in his life. He walked me to the end of the aisle where I met Spencer. Spencer was a ball of nerves. My bridal party was made up of Stella, Olivia, Kennedy and my niece Layla. Spencer had his two cousins Henry and Wyatt, Owen and

John-O on his groomsmen team. His nephew was the ring bearer and JV was our flower girl. Everyone looked so amazing in the colors I picked out. When Reverend Czar pronounced us husband and wife, Spencer leaned over to kiss me and I started crying like a baby as we headed back up the aisle to greet our guests.

After the wedding, we rode in the limo back to take pictures and then arrived at the house for the reception. We quickly found out that the DJ was late. Spencer slammed the limo door and shoved the photographer out of the way as he tried to take a picture as we exited the limo. I begged Spencer to calm down while we went inside to take a break from everything that was happening. Within ten minutes the music had started and my brother Will was on the mic as MC kicking off the festivities and everything seemed to get back on track

Dominic's mom made our cake, a beautiful three-tier staircase design. I was surprised at how beautiful it was. We didn't have a lot of money, but I was proud of how it all came together. It proved to me that love can make anything happen. The dance floor was the blacktop of our driveway in the back. Everyone danced the night away and had a great time. At the end of the night we said our goodbyes, took the limo into Manhattan and spent the weekend at the Marriott Marquis in the center of Times Square. We ate in the restaurant on the top of the hotel called the Top of the View that spins while you dine. We weren't able to go away because I was graduating from Old Westbury with my Bachelor's degree the following weekend and had finals that week. At that moment, I felt like I was on top of the world. Marrying my junior high school sweetheart was one of the best things that had ever happened to me.

A few weeks after Spencer and I got married he attempted to reach Diana to see the kids but had not heard back from her by the end of the second day. She hadn't allowed them to come to the wedding. When he didn't hear from her, he started to get nervous. At the time, Diana was in a relationship with a guy named Noah that we all knew from high school. She was living with him at an apartment in Queens. Spencer decided to make an unannounced trip to her apartment and when we got there we ran into Noah and asked where Diana was. It was clear that when we asked about her, he was hiding something. He said that he had not seen her and it appeared that she had taken everything she had including Spencer's kids and all her things. We found out a later that she took the kids to Florida to live without notifying Spencer. This is when the hell started...

For several weeks, Spencer had no idea where the kids were and Diana was not in touch with anyone so we had no idea where she went. Spencer hired a private investigator that did the work to track her down and eventually, he was able to figure out and confirm that she took the kids and moved to Florida where she had some family members. During the time he could not find his kids, Spencer was not the same. He was very angry, frustrated and disappointed. He focused all of his time and energy on figuring out how to get Diana to bring the kids back to NY. Once he located her physical address he went to court and filed an order to have her served and brought back to NY. Once the court documents were filed, he had to pay a process server to get her the court papers and eventually they tracked her down and she received the court papers. Within nine to twelve months, Diana came back to NY for the court date. The court ordered her to move back to NY. The judge also granted Spencer specific visitation rights. This included being able to have the kids every other weekend and split visitation rights on specific holidays directed by the court. That day the judge allowed the kids to stay with us. We were so happy to see Sydney and Samuel. He cried when he saw them since it was the first time after almost a year. They were only 8 and 3 at the time.

Sydney and Samuel were able to stay with us for a few days before they had to leave and Diana made her arrangements to move back to NY. Once she came back, she and Spencer worked out their visitation matters. It was frustrating at times, however, I tried my best to stay out of the way of the two of them. Every time they talked there was some serious animosity and their regular communication was quite argumentative. What I did every time was remind Spencer that the kids would get older very quickly and that they would one day be old enough to make their own decisions to visit and be with him the way he hoped. I continuously tried to get him to focus on the relationship with his children, however, in the midst of so much anger it is very difficult to see past the current storm.

BLESSINGS

10

Planned Parenthood

❖•❖•————————❖•❖•❖•❖•❖————————•❖•❖

My most important goal at this point was to work with Spencer to integrate his children with my children as successfully as possible, the same way I saw my mother do it for many years with my father and all of his many children. This was a lifestyle I was very familiar and comfortable with since my father had so many children that were not my mother's. When you are younger you might say to yourself (as I even did), "When I grow up I am going to have two or three children." I am sure my father never woke up and said I am going to have at least 18 children. At least I hope not, but that is what happened.

My Dad's story is a fascinating one. He was born and raised in Denbigh (Denby) on the island of Jamaica. He did a lot of running around with many women for years until he settled down and married my mother. My father and the mother of my oldest sister Lillian, were close in age and both were in their twenties when she was born. Lillian's mother also had a daughter from her second marriage who was Lillian's little sister. Since I was also Lillian's sister on her father's side, I called her sister my sister for many years, so we shared a sister. We were practically the same age, only three months apart, which meant that my mother and her mother were pregnant at the same time. My father also had five children with another woman who pulled up to his house in Jamaica and dropped all five off at my grandmother's house and she said, "Here, they now belong to you." Daddy's son Howie had yet another mother. Dad also had two daughters with women from Canada. We went to visit Canada a lot because my Aunt Rhoda lived there and it also gave him a chance to visit with his daughters. His one daughter Pam died about 10 or 15 years ago of cancer. So far that is 11 children I have mentioned of my fathers.

More recently, probably in the year 2010, I met another brother and his family. His name is Carlton and he's a teacher. He has a sister named Audrey. This family found us through a picture book that featured my parents' pictures in the early pages. Carlton's co-worker came across the book that showed a picture of my parents next to the three coffins that they buried their three children in, including my mother's son Junior. The book was called "No Grave Can Hold My Body Down". The book described the designs of coffins and how they have changed over time in post-colonial Jamaica. As a result of finding this book, my brother pursued finding his Dad who I am not sure he had ever met. I can't forget Dennis and Joy who died in the car accident in 1968 with Junior. In the end, my father had four children with my mother, including Junior. After my mother he re-married again and supposedly had another son named Eric with his wife, but we were never sure if he was truly his son. So far that is 18, including me.

My mother shared another story with me that there was another daughter (who I never heard of but who may be close to my age) by the name of Jackie. Apparently her mom was Chinese, and her name is Lupi Lee. She says she never met her, but explained a story of her mom contacting my Dad when mom and Dad were getting married. She needed money from him for an insurance policy for the girl. My mother said my Dad never gave her the money and she wasn't sure how she received their mailing address, but she was attempting to reach her to finance raising the child. Having this many children can be very complicated and at times can cause chaos however this is the path my father chose.

Planning how much of a family you are going to have sounds like a nice thing to do, but it also seems as if it would be quite the challenge. Aborting two children because I was not ready to be a parent was the most devastating experience I ever had in my life. I always ask myself what would have happened if I had planned ahead for parenthood. What would have happened if I was aborted? I ask myself this question often since life would not have been an option for me if that were the case. If I had to do it all over again, I would certainly have been smarter about the choices I made related to my sexual behavior. I certainly would have been more vigilant with the use of birth control to avoid the feelings of guilt that had been harbored in my soul for many years.

This brings me back to a time when Spencer and I were back together and first starting out. I was working in Melville, NY at Career Blazers Learning Center as an Admissions Rep. I would go to local government agency offices and attempt to get their workers signed up for re-employment programs with us. These programs offered them training for a certain amount of weeks, usually in technology programs like CNA, (Certified Network Administrator) and help desk support. I had been doing this sales work for a short time and then realized it wasn't for me. At the same time, I made a decision to start my Master's in Social Work at Adelphi.

When I look back on my academic life, smoking weed and not attending class wasted two whole years at Virginia State. I then redeemed myself with my father and received my Associate's degree from Durham Technical Community College in North Carolina which put me back on the right track. I had successfully received my Bachelor's degree from Old Westbury in 1994 after failing out of Virginia State. Once I made the decision to go to Adelphi, I was beginning to think seriously about what type of work I wanted to do as a career and not just to have a job anymore.

I was in my late twenties at the time and figured it was finally the time for me to get purposeful about my career since I took a different path and focused on relationships and having kids first. This is not the typical path to go, but whose path is really typical? Some people go to school, get a good job, then get married, and then have babies. I did it the other way around, but this journey didn't make me any less prepared for what life had in store. I went to school, met guys, had babies, finished school, and then got married. From there I went back to focusing on my career and furthering my education. Everyone's path is distinct and specific for them and we are not in a race to the finish. If your mindset it to compete with others, then you are not on the right track. Everyone has their own road to travel. The goal should be to have a purposeful journey while offering help to others on the way.

I applied to Adelphi and got into their Master of Social Work (MSW) program. I was extremely excited. At this point in my life I thought I wanted to become a Social Worker. I was sure I wanted to help people; I didn't know how or where, I just knew that is what I wanted to do. I started the program and before finishing the first year of the MSW, you have to take on an internship. You have to work a certain amount of hours in a social work field to supplement your school work as a requirement for the degree.

When the list of places came around for students to select where they wanted to do their internships, none of them struck a chord for me at all. Many of them were situations where you would be working with the developmentally disabled, with senior citizens or other areas that didn't connect for me. Instead I went out on a limb, even though there was no association or contract with this organization; I decided to contact Planned Parenthood to see if they would allow me to do my internship with them. I wrote them a letter and surprisingly enough they called me in for an interview. I met with the person in charge, told her my interest in helping young people and they liked me. I would be getting college credit and I wouldn't be paid for the work, so they offered me the internship opportunity. I was able to start right away.

I had prior experience with Planned Parenthood, as a patient. I had gone there a few times for counseling when I was trying to determine if and when I would have an abortion. I never actually had the abortion procedure done at Planned Parenthood since the two procedures I had were both done in the hospital, however I recall going there and feeling that it was a supportive place to talk to someone. Here is where you can get help with understanding birth control and other sexual health options.

I was scheduled twice a week and all day on Saturday once I began my internship. I was taught about the birth control mechanisms available and operational procedures of the site. Most of the time I was there, I was counseling young woman who were coming in to determine if they were going to make a decision to have an abortion.

I was not there to help them make the decision; I was there to explain what the procedure would be like. The process was very intimate and stressful.

There are a few kinds of in-clinic abortion procedures. The clinicians would tell them which type was right for them depending on how far along the person was into the pregnancy. Suction abortion, which is also called vacuum aspiration, is the most common type of in-clinic abortion. It uses gentle suction to empty the uterus. It's usually used until about 14-16 weeks after the last period the woman has experienced. Dilation and Evacuation (D&E) is another kind of in-clinic abortion procedure. It uses suction and medical tools to empty your uterus. You can get a D&E later in a pregnancy than aspiration abortion -- usually if it has been 16 weeks or longer since your last period. Unfortunately, I have experienced both types.

After several weeks of working at Planned Parenthood and meeting what felt like hundreds of women, it was starting to weigh on me. Protesters were out in front of my building in Hempstead every time I came to work. These protesters were people who were against abortion and the use of birth control in general. Once I got past the door, I saw at least 20 experiences where a young woman would come in for the procedure alone. Someone would drop them off, usually a friend, and just leave them and no one would be there to support them during the actual procedure. When it was time for them to go inside the procedure room, they were so afraid they would almost always ask me to go inside with them. Each time I went in with them because I knew what it might have felt like to go through it alone at such a desperate, lonely and scary time. Both times when I was having this experience myself my mother was there with me, although not by her choice or mine. I recognized that she was very worried about me and wanted to make sure I was getting the best care I could get even in the worst circumstances of my life where she wanted to kill me herself.

I had gone in the room with woma many times. I held their hands and tried to get them to calm down and breathe. They were never put to sleep. The room was white and cold, with several tools that you could almost never decipher what they were designed to do. The worst part was to hear the vacuum machine go on and then you wait for the vaginal tool to be inserted inside the uterus. I think the noise from the vacuum was the worst part, and then the pain you felt afterwards because once the embryo was extracted you would begin to get your period and the worst cramps you have ever had in your life! All the procedures were done while you were awake. Many of these women were relieved after this experience, but many also walked away with the same feeling that I had which was a heavy feeling of guilt that didn't go away easily.

After about eight weeks of working with Planned Parenthood I made a decision to leave the internship. The struggle of coming face-to-face again three times a week with what was the worst experience of my life was taking its toll on me. In addition, after doing more research on what kind of career life I could have as a social worker, I often wondered if I would be financially stable with a social worker's salary while I already had two kids. I finally gave up and called Planned Parenthood quits, and at the same time dropped out of the Master's program. As a result of this decision, I became depressed for several months. Dropping out of school made me feel like a failure. I had come so far. My father believed in me again since I got my degree and I was doing so well in my mind. I eventually snapped out of it and moved on and got past the decision to drop out. Clearly it is okay to change direction in your choice of major and your career goals and try something else. Just as long as you keep going after your dreams, you're fine.

Not long after quitting the Master's program at Adelphi, I quit my job at Career Blazers too, and took a risk and started some temporary work. My first temp assignment was in 1997 at a Long Island firm called CMP Media, which was a publishing company. I was able to get a job as a temporary Human Resources Assistant supporting a woman by the name of Angela Kay. Angela was the HR Director for the Operations division of the organization I supported. There were two other HR Directors at her level that supported the Finance and Electronic teams. I was doing so well in the temporary assignment that they hired me full-time after two weeks. This is how I got my start in Human Resources.

I remained there for two years and really enjoyed my work and learning everything there is to know about HR from the ground up. After getting promoted into a more senior role supporting the new Chief HR Officer, Mary Hill, I truly loved what I was doing. I would always complete projects quickly and ask for more work from Mary. I was constantly looking for the next visible, important project. Based on my level of engagement on some projects and not on others, like the administrative work for her, she didn't think I was fully committed to being an Administrative Assistant so she recommended that I expand my horizons and look out into Manhattan for other opportunities. I took her advice and did just that. She and I both thought it was time for me to move on to something bigger and better and I appreciated her for having that vision.

I interviewed for my first job in NYC based on answering an ad in the newspaper. That was an old school way of applying for jobs. No one does that anymore. Everything is social media driven these days. After three interviews I showcased my skill set on how to maneuver the internet, which was brand new at the time. I was able to show them everything I knew about how to access clients through warm methods of contact. I showed this team of white men in suits how I could use the resources available on the World Wide Web to help them recruit their insurance agents which was very appealing to them. Shortly after the interview, I was offered the position as a Recruitment Specialist at the Equitable Life Assurance Society of

NY. They eventually changed their name to AXA Equitable and then to just AXA. This was a very exciting time in my life. It was where my income really began to increase. Every time I filled an insurance agent position I would receive a $500 bonus in addition to my annual salary.

After the first year in this non-traditional HR role as an Insurance Recruiter for AXA the position was eliminated, but then I was quickly transferred into a true Human Resources position as an Employee Relations Specialist. Here I met Carolyn Gray, who taught me everything I know about employee relations and investigating employee complaints. I managed all kinds of claims including employees complaining about managers, managers complaining about employees, sexual harassment and discrimination claims. I did this work for two years and then September 11, 2001 happened and changed NYC forever.

I was on my way to work on that fateful morning of 9/11. The E train was running a little slow, which is not that unusual. But that day it felt a little more eerie, almost like it was moving backwards or in slow motion. I got off at my stop at 53rd street and 7th avenue in midtown. I approached my office at 51st and 6th, and walked into the office at about 8:45 am to the phone actively ringing. It was my husband Spencer calling me. He also worked in Manhattan not far from me and literally down the block. He had been at work since 6 am at the NBA where he was the Chef of their corporate cafeteria. In a very somber voice he said, "Babe, did you hear what happened downtown?" I said "No, what?" At that point he told me a plane had hit the World Trade Center. He said this solemnly and slowly because he knew my sister Lillian worked in Building 2 at the World Trade Center. I was in utter shock and stood still for a moment trying to understand what he was saying to me. At that point I freaked out and started crying and panicking.

By this time Lillian had worked at the Twin Towers for almost 30 years. I had gone there often as a child to visit her in her office. She worked on the 92nd floor and it was an adventure every time to go up in the elevators practically to the top floor to go and meet her. I never really liked it there because I was somewhat afraid of heights and the building sometimes swayed when you were close to the top when it was windy, or if you just stood still and connected with it. You could feel it. I always remember being afraid when I was up there. It was a feeling I will never forget. Then the second plane hit. At that point I ran into the conference room and told everyone on my floor what was happening. No one else appeared to know the city was falling down around us. Since we didn't have TVs in our offices, you had to go to the conference room with where there was a television to recognize what was happening in the outside world.

After the two planes each crashed into a building, both buildings collapsed into a cloud of dust shortly afterwards, one by one. It was surreal. It was like a really bad movie that would not stop playing.

People were running and screaming into the streets. It was like nothing we had ever seen in this lifetime. At first the news was reporting that they thought it was an accident, but it quickly became clear it was a terrorist attack on the United States. Later on we found out that a terrorist regime named Al Queda was behind these awful attacks.

Not long after this, Spencer came to meet me at my office and we attempted to leave the city together but all the trains were shut down. There was no cell phone service and after several attempts we hadn't been able to get a hold of my sister to see if she was okay. I was pregnant with my son Max at the time, which was the first planned pregnancy I ever had. I was scared, anxious and nervous and didn't want anything to upset this pregnancy. By then I knew Spencer and I were going to have a boy since Spencer and I had four kids already (three girls and 1 boy) we wanted to know this babies sex. The day I went for the sonogram I was with Princess and Spencer's nephew and immediately you could see his manhood peeking out on the sonogram. I was so excited to be having my first son.

At around 2:30 pm that day I finally got word that my sister was late to work and got stuck going back to Long Island through Queens. But more importantly, she was okay and she was alive. When the trains started running again, Spencer and I were eventually able to get the E train to Jamaica and then transfer to the Long Island railroad to get home. The trains were packed solid and everyone was still in shock about the terror that was happening around us. I went straight to my sister Lillian's house in Uniondale and still couldn't believe this ALL wasn't just a dream... When the incident was finally reported in its entirety, four planes had crashed; two into the world trade center, one into the Pentagon in D.C. and one into a field in Pennsylvania where some kick ass passengers probably beat the terrorist's asses before it went down. At the end of the day we lost almost 3000 people that day, including average workers and first responders. New York would never be the same again. Some are still acquiring diseases including cancer and dying from the after effects of the debris that fell all around downtown Manhattan. Many of those were helping to clean up and had no idea of the toxins in the air. Unfortunately, those people who lost their lives will never be able to live another day and all they did was get up that morning and go about their normal routines of life like we all do daily. Waking up, getting dressed and going to work became a deadly assignment. RIP. When you think about challenges you face and how difficult it is to get past tough experiences in your life, take a moment to think about all the people who have passed away ahead of you noting that they don't have another chance to go on that job interview or re-take the test that was failed, and so many other opportunities that you have the chance to make up do over again. Keep on going after your dreams. Three months after 9/11 on December 9th, I gave birth to our healthy baby boy Maximus who has been nothing but an angel since the day he was born.

11

The Real World

The real world is an interesting thing. We are all here living life from our own perspectives; each of us walking around in our own shoes and experiencing all the various activities life has to offer, a social construct of sorts. The more interesting part is the way we all deal with the many challenges that cross our paths. One of those challenges is the death of a loved one. For many years I wasn't really sure what it was like to lose someone that was close to me. As I write, that will all change.

Reality shows were introduced through cable television going back to the first show I can remember which I think received its credit as the first reality show ever created back in 1992 called "The Real World". On this show, seven to eight young adults were picked to temporarily live in a new city together in one house while being filmed non-stop. The series was documented in its early years for portraying issues of that time, of young-adulthood focused on its core audience of a similar age, portraying actions such as sex, prejudice, religion, abortion, illness, sexuality, AIDS, death, politics, and substance abuse. Later it turned into a showcase for immaturity and irresponsible behavior, but not before hundreds of other similar types of reality shows came after it. Reality shows displayed real life on television in a way people had never seen it before. It became a fascinating trend, but it was not the real world. The real world offers real things like heartbreak, real decision-making, and death.

The first real significant deaths I felt in my life were the abortion experiences I'd had. Some of you might read this and say, how could you consider that a death if you CHOSE to abort a child? Some might look at it as murder. Some might look at is as a last resort or as no choice and still others might say you can relate because it happened to you, too. If you've been through it you know this disgusting feeling of guilt, depression and sadness that comes with it. Some who had the experience may have felt relieved, like a huge weight was taken off of your back and shoulders. The experience for me was definitely a loss. A death like no other and, possibly, why I have developed this black hole in my soul, this six-foot-deep grave that I believe will always be there. Since then I have experienced several other significant losses in my life. Loss is a given, and it is imminent. How we deal with loss though is the more important test of life. I want to share the stories of a few of the great people who I have lost in this life.

Vanessa

When I was pregnant with my son Max while working at AXA, I had a friend by the name of Vanessa who was our front desk receptionist for the 7th floor of Human Resources. Vanessa was a lovely woman. She had the most beautiful spirit anyone could ever have. She was a light brown black woman, about 5'6", medium weight and dressed up like she was going to church every day. She had beautiful dresses and skirts and blouses. She wore trendy eyeglasses and when she greeted people at the front desk she called everyone sweetheart, baby and my love and hugged everyone. She was like a beautiful Auntie, or older cousin to me. We became really close and spent lots of time socializing and going out to lunch together. Some days we stayed inside and watched All My Children on the television in the conference room. We'd bring our lunch and keep it really dark so no one saw us or came in and every day that we could, we'd watch this soap at 1:00 p.m. When I was pregnant, I used to crave french fries. I ate them practically every day so she nicknamed my unborn baby "Frenchie" before Max was even born.

After about a year, Vanessa got promoted and moved out of HR into another department on the 11th floor. As a result, I didn't get to see her as often as I used to. At one point she got sick and was out of work on FML (Family Medical Leave). The leave eventually extended out to a long-term period of time. Longer than I thought it would. I checked on her from time to time and eventually found out she had cancer and that it was too late for treatment. I was not that familiar with what cancer was back then, but I knew I didn't like it if Vanessa had it. She had some type of esophageal cancer that started with feelings of indigestion.

After a few months passed I received word that Vanessa had passed away. I was devastated. How could someone who was eating lunch with me almost every day be dead now? Well, I was not alone in my sadness. Many of us at work were struck by her death since she touched so many lives in the office with her kindness. Her funeral was held at a church in Mount Vernon. I attended with Carolyn Gray and I promised I would never forget her. A few months later I sent her husband a personal letter describing what a beautiful person she was, which I am sure he already knew. It is so important that we cherish the lives of our loved ones who have gone away in the hope of rising again.

JC

The next significant loss I experienced in my life was that of my stepfather, JC. After my parents were divorced back in the 80's, my mother dated JC who she knew from her time in Jamaica when she was young. While she and my Dad were calling it quits, she started talking to JC on the phone in the morning before I went to school. I remember this going back to when I was in the 6th grade. I would be headed out to go meet Anthony to take that walk down to California

Ave. School and before I left I would kiss her goodbye and she would be on the phone with him. I didn't see it as unusual since I was so young. Shortly thereafter, she moved out and went to live with my aunt and uncle in Hempstead before eventually getting her own apartment with JC. They subsequently got married. I was not allowed to go to the wedding. I assume it was because my father was still pissed. I saw pictures and got the 411 later on in life. For a while, I saw JC as the reason for my parents breaking up, but found out much later on that it was more than that and not that easy to blame him for the break-up of my parents.

Relevant to their break-up, my mom always talked about my Dad as an old fashioned man in his later years. I assume he must have been exhausted from having all those kids! Whatever the case may be, he didn't like to travel. When he and my mom did go out to family parties he would drink, abuse alcohol, carry on, yell, and preach about all the things we all should know and do better. Then I am sure he would pass out. We would also get our asses kicked from time to time by him. My brothers more so than me, but I got my licks too. I was incredibly afraid of my father and did my best not to do anything to make him mad or angry with me. Whatever I did do that I wasn't supposed to do was kept a secret to the best of my ability. I remember him once tying up my brothers on the support pole in the basement because they had disobeyed him. One by one they were tied up with their hands on the pole and beaten with the belt. I screamed and cried for them because I thought I was next. I got it, but not as bad as they did.

Eventually, I understand that my mom just didn't want to deal with being unhappy anymore since she wanted to travel, visit with family and just go out and have a good time without all the drama. When my mom left and married JC, I stayed and lived with my Dad. For many years, I responded to her leaving my Dad as leaving me, and that caused a great separation between us; I resented her. Although she asked me at the time if I wanted to come and live with her, in my mind I wondered when is it a child's choice to pick which parent they want to live with? I learned later on that my father was not allowing my mom to take me with her so whether I wanted it or she wanted it, it would not have happened. I wondered how she could leave me as a young girl with my father and three boys in the house since by then my older sister Victoria, who is my mother's only other daughter, had already left and got married. She was my mother's daughter with another man before she married my father. Victoria came to the US a little while after my parents got settled here. Victoria was 10 years older than me. She had a lighter complexion than me and was chunky, cute and very bossy. To her I was more like a little doll than her sister. She dragged me along with her wherever she went whether she liked it or not. She made cupcakes for me for school functions and did my hair for school when my mother was not home to do it. My oldest sister Lillian on my father's side who is 20 years older than me didn't live very far away. She was just down the block in the same town. Having her close by brought me a lot of comfort however I was too young at the time to really talk to either of them. I mean really talk about boys, clothes and life. I looked at Lillian as a mom for many years, and still do. I would have been devastated if she had died on 9/11.

With all that said, after many years of feeling some hatred for my stepfather coming into the picture and seemingly breaking up my family, I got to know him better and realized he was not the bad person I was portraying him to be. He was a very loving grandfather to my children; he gave us great advice about life, played the best old school reggae music you could ever hear in the world, and he was a man of God. Step parents are not so bad if you get to know them for who they are and not for the experience that brought them into your life.

At the time of JC's passing, I was going through a rough time with being deathly afraid to fly. Back in about 1991, I mentioned having worked for a company called Tower Airlines. Tower Air was co-founded, majority owned, and managed by Morris K. Nachtomi, an Israeli citizen who had immigrated to the United States who I knew and would see all the time and talk to at work. He spent 30 years with El Al (another Israeli airline), before he moved to New York to start another airline. After this airline shut down, Mr. Nachtomi acquired the "Tower" brand from a packaged tour agency called Tower Travel

Corporation. Tower Air began charter service in 1983 and served a number of international destinations, with a focus on charter flights to Israel. We flew a Boeing 747-100 which is a huge airliner. I had some good times working for them as a Reservations Agent at JFK, eventually being promoted to the Supervisor on the Tel Aviv desk. We didn't fly to many places when I was there, but we did have regular flights to Israel, Miami, San Juan, Puerto Rico and Brazil. I even booked our Spanish-speaking customers on flights to Puerto Rico and Miami because I knew enough Spanish to make a reservation. I would say "A Donde vas" and it could only be Miami or Puerto Rico, because not many Spanish people were going to Israel, "Que dia, a que hora, cuantos pasajeros y el total es"…I knew my dinero in Spanish too.

When you work for an airline, one of the best benefits they offer is free flights. I never really liked to fly so I didn't use the benefit but my mom used to fly to Miami often because my sister Victoria got divorced and moved there. I didn't fly for many years after this except that one time when the children, JV and Princess, were sent to Jamaica for the summer to spend time with their grandparents. They flew with the flight attendants and Spencer and I went back to get them. The other times they went, my mom brought them back. A good seven years went by before I flew again. I gave up opportunities for work to travel, including turning down a trip to Paris that I will always regret.

In August of 2008 I got word from my mother that JC had a stroke, was in the hospital and a few days later he passed away. At that moment I knew I was going to have to face my fears again head on. I planned a trip to Jamaica with my mother's best friend. We left on 8/26. My niece and my brother Will also met me there and we were able to help my mother with the arrangements and the memorial for JC. The service had to be delayed due to a hurricane that washed away a local bridge that stunted a lot of travel into the area. I came back on 9/4, but not before having to circle JFK like 20 times because there was so much air traffic. I was so proud of myself for getting past the fear this time and supporting my mom during this very tough time in her life.

Brooke

Another significant loss in my world was the deaths of my two sisters in law; Brooke the younger sister and Josie who was the oldest. Spencer has three sisters, including his third sister June who is the middle child. I have known his sisters since I was very young when Spencer and I first dated back in November of 1982. We lived around the corner from each other in our hometown of Uniondale, NY. If you walked to the end of my corner and made a right on Manor Pkwy and then a left onto Marvin Ave. you could hop the fence and be at Spencer's house on Walton Ave. in no time.

Most of the time when I went to his house it was secretively because he didn't want his family to know we were seeing each other. He was a very private person. If I did get "seen" there it wouldn't necessarily be as his girlfriend. I recall seeing his sisters there from time to time. Most times they were upstairs in their room across the hall from his and I would just say hi quickly and go into his room. He would explain to me that they were having trouble walking and that he had to go with his mom and take them to doctors all the time, sometimes out of state to see what was going on. Later, it turned out that they had become immobile and lived most of their lives unable to walk, paralyzed from the waist down. They had to use wheelchairs to get around and needed help to do most things including eating and using the bathroom. The doctors labeled it a disease called Fried Reich's ataxia (FA). They really didn't know for sure what it was, but like most things, it had to get a "label". Fried Reich's ataxia (FA) is an autosomal recessive inherited disease that causes progressive damage to the nervous system. It manifests in initial symptoms of poor coordination such as gait disturbance; it can also lead to scoliosis, heart disease and diabetes, but does not affect cognitive function. Its incidence in the general population is roughly 1 in 50,000 (but it hit two sisters living in the same house). Symptoms typically begin sometime between the ages of 5 to 15 years, but this started for them after high school. Late onset FA may occur in the twenties or thirties. Symptoms include any combination, but not necessarily all, of the following: muscle weakness in the arms and legs, loss of coordination, vision impairment, hearing impairment, slurred speech, curvature of the spine (scoliosis), high plantar arches (pes cavus deformity of the foot), diabetes, and heart disorders. Vision impairment came very much later in life for Josie, but never Brooke. They never had diabetes, hearing impairment or slurred speech, so the diagnosis seemed definitely inappropriate.

After a bad break up between Spencer's mom and their stepfather, they eventually moved out of Uniondale to Freeport, also to Roosevelt, where I lived with them at one point for a short time and eventually Baldwin. Not long after they moved to Baldwin we did too, less than a mile from them. It was important to Spencer that we stayed closed to his family. I always admired him for this love and care he had for his family. After many years of Brooke and Josie living with their illness, it eventually took a turn for the worse, for Brooke first.

A year after her 50th birthday, she went into the hospital with symptoms of chest pains and difficulty breathing. After getting checked in and staying there a few days they recognized her disability, ran a series of tests, saw that there was water on her lungs and determined that there was not much more they could do for her based on her current condition. At the time, my mother in law was out of town in Grenada. No one wanted to worry her so we waited until she came back to tell her that Brooke was released to go home into hospice care.

When Brooke came home from the hospital in April of 2012, she was fully aware of what was happening. She was engaged with all of us with the nurse who took us all through the hospice care process and what would take place while she was under this care. Brooke sat up in her wheelchair in her short shorts and tank top and hair beautifully combed. She always looked her best no matter how she felt.

Hospice Care is designed to give supportive care to people in the final phase of a terminal illness and the focus is on comfort and quality of life, rather than cure. The goal is to enable patients to be comfortable and free of pain, so they live each day as fully as possible. Aggressive methods of pain control may also be used at this stage of the process, and later on they were.

Brooke was getting nursing care around the clock and slowly, day-by-day; you could see her physically deteriorating. By the time her next birthday came around on October 15th, she was barely able to speak. In her last days, all we wanted to do was be with her and do the things we could to try to make her happy, to make her smile. Brooke had a friend who came to visit from Grenada who did just that. Her friend happened to be the Ambassador for Grenada, so she had a few important contacts in her rolodex.

Everyone who knew Brooke knew the love and adoration that she had for George Clooney. Brooke's friend knew this love as well and reached out directly to Morgan Freeman who made a connection to George Clooney on her behalf. She explained that Brooke was living her last days and asked if he would spend some time with her on the phone, and he did! He was shooting a movie in the Midwest and made time to contact her and speak to her. He told her that he loved her and she said her last words by telling him she loved him too. The call was recorded and it was a very touching moment. There wasn't a dry eye in the room.

Approximately one month later in 2012, super storm Sandy hit which took a toll on Long Island. As a result of the loss of power, we had to relocate Brooke to the hospital for oxygen since her current machine was electric. She was only there for a few hours. She came back home equipped with a proper tank that didn't need electrical power to run. A day or so later on 11/1/2012, which happens to be the date Spencer and me originally became a couple in 1982, Brooke took her last breath in the middle of the night at approximately 2 am. That date will always have meaning to us. The entire family was there. We said our prayers with her and not long after, called the funeral home to come and pick her body up. The worst part of this was watching the two men come in and take her body out of the house. It was a very difficult moment for everyone, but mainly for her mom. We had a memorial service at our church for her two weeks later and we honored her the best way we could knowing that our lives will never be the same without her.

Don

Less than eight months later, Spencer's father Don, my father-in-law, passed away. Spencer had not been in touch with his father for many years until more recently. The story of Don based on Spencer's account was that he was a seaman, and after traveling on the seas for many years as a drug dealer, he was busted and was banned from the U.S. About five years before Brooke passed away, he came to New York for the first time in many years to everyone's surprise. Don was tall and brown-skinned, nothing like I pictured him to look since Spencer was so light-skinned and was of average height. He took all of his looks from his mom since they looked so much alike. I had heard many stories about him from Spencer, and from Spencer's Mom, Mary. She called him all kinds of names and said he left her and her children to run off with another woman who he eventually married. After all those years though, I believe she still truly loved him.

I was so interested in finding out what happened to them and who he really was after all these years since it all seemed to be so mysterious that he was not in their lives. In August of 1997, I wrote him a letter to break the silence and here is what it said;

Dear Don,

    Hello and how are you? I hope this letter finds you and your family in good health. It was very nice to be able to talk to you for the first time this past weekend. Just to give you some background, Spencer and I have known each other now for almost 17 years. We grew up together in the same neighborhood in Uniondale, New York. We shared a relationship for a few years and then I moved out of state to go to college. During that time Spencer was involved in another relationship with a woman named Diane and they had two children; Sydney - 10 and Samuel - 5. I also had a daughter outside of our marriage named JV, who is 8. Once I moved back to Long Island both Spencer and I separated from our previous relationships and got back together (true love right?). Anyhow, I figured I should give you some of our history together that you missed. We've been married for 3 1/2 years and I'm very sorry that you were not able to be a part of it. I enclosed some photos from the wedding for you to see. We also have a daughter together named Princess, who is now 3 years old. Although you have been separated from Spencer and his sisters for some time he has never forgotten about you. The strain of Spencer being the only man at his house has been very difficult for him for many years. He has been working since high school to support his mom and sisters and ever since we got married there has been a lot of tension between us. They have been back-and-forth between speaking and not speaking to me, but no matter what I do, they have refused to accept me. I try not to take it personal because I do understand him being the only son to his mother, but I really did try hard so we could all get along, but nothing seems to work. I'm at the point where I cannot make them like me, but it still keeps Spencer in the middle. I encourage him to visit his family and to always keep in touch with his mom. Luckily, we have a very strong bond in our relationship and we have been very successful in dealing with a lot of pressure on us. Besides that, you also know that Spencer has been working in the culinary field and he recently finished school at a two-year college for the culinary arts. Cooking is something Spencer is great at and he hopes to one day have his own catering business or restaurant. He works for one of the top restaurants in the country called Tavern on the Green. He's fairly new there and is not 100% sure if he'll stay, but he's trying it out. I work in the human resources department for a publishing company here called CMP Media that produces computer magazines. I have my Bachelor's degree in Sociology, but have found human resources to be more interesting. I am hoping that encouraging Spencer to call you this past Sunday will allow you two to make up for the lost time. You have our number now and you should feel free to call. It might not be easy to try and develop a new relationship with Spencer, but if you both are willing you never know what can happen. I think life is too short to hold any grudges. Anyway I really enjoyed talking to you on the phone and I hope we will hear from you again soon. I look forward to receiving some pictures of you as well. Take care.

Sincerely,

Lisa.

I don't know if this letter was written on Spencer's behalf or on my own. From a selfish perspective, I wanted Spencer's father to know all about our life together and that he was able to be successful without him in his life. Several years later, when Max was very young, Don came back to NY for the first time after many years. It was like a reunion of sorts for the family, but there were obvious mixed feelings for seeing him again. He attempted to rebuild his relationship with my mother-in-law, Mary. They laughed, fought, and cried together in the process. They also came to Max's soccer games and drank lots of vino together. It was an interesting time and fascinating to see them interacting with each other. Don aka "Dads" came back to New York two or three times after the first time. The last time he came he broke the news to my mother-in-law that he had prostate cancer. We started to wonder if that is why he came back around in the first place, to make amends before he passed away. Once he went back to TriniDad that last time, he passed away. Mary,

Spencer, me, Princess and my mother took the trip to Canouan, a very small island off the Grenadines where he is from, to attend his funeral and bury him.

We landed in Barbados first to meet my Mom who was coming from Jamaica via Antigua, then transferred to a smaller, louder plane that took us over to Canouan. It was shocking to me that I was able to get my mother to join us, but I told her I would purchase her ticket and she seemed excited for the opportunity to join us. We stayed there for about four days, attended the funeral and finally met her…Spencer's stepmother, who I had heard so much about. In the eyes of Mary, she was the woman that stole her husband, sickened her children and turned her life upside down. I also saw Spencer's little brother who I had met once before when he came to New York. My mother-in-law was a strong woman and went through a great deal of pain based on Dads choices, leaving her, not providing for the family as he should have, and disenfranchising himself from them. Through it all she came through a terrible storm and showed us all how resilient she was as a single mother of four children.

The funeral was well attended. We were able to see his body as the family one last time before the service started. He looked stoic and peaceful in the coffin wearing a black suit. He was clean shaven and neat, but it was a bitter sweet moment to have to come to an end this way. After the service we escorted his body out of the little Catholic Church on the hill and followed the parade of people walking down the hill to his final resting place a short walk away overlooking the waterfront of Canouan. We watched intently as the diggers shoveled the dirt to the side and placed his coffin into the six-foot grave. After the grave was dug and the coffin was placed, the diggers built a stone castle around the grave. They placed what seemed like hundreds of stones of various sizes on top of one another along the entire perimeter of the grave. In the end it was standing at about five feet tall. On top of the completed structure, a painting of a boat was placed on top of the grave to signify his time as a seaman while everyone then placed flowers on the structure. The church choir, made up of several older Caribbean women, began singing church hymns. They all had Bibles in their hands. Everyone joined in where they could and knew the words. *Amazing grace, how sweet the sound, that saved a wretch like me...I once was lost but now I'm found, twas blind but now I see.* I took a few videos in order to share them with June once we returned. She couldn't bring herself to make the trip and watch as father was buried.

As a result of the funeral, I was finally able to see Spencer's small island where he spent time with his grandmother, Mami Berti, at Petit Martinique. We took a small island boat to get to it. The island is about two miles in width and one mile in length. We toured the island by truck and by foot and were able to get around the entire island in less than two hours. We then headed back to Canouan which is not that much bigger. This was a very special trip for all of us.

John-O

Another significant death in my life was the death of our friend John-O. John-O was Spencer's best friend since junior high school. He lived on Lawrence St. which was just down the block from where we grew up in Uniondale right past Roy Rogers, an old fast food restaurant in our neighborhood. Spencer and John did some significant running around together. John was a tall, medium to heavy built guy, brown skinned and filled with the lyrics of a poet. He loved to rap and play basketball, which were his two favorite things to do. He never went pro, but he did eventually become a teacher, which was in his genes. Both of his parents were teachers. His mom was one of the sweetest people I have ever met. She was a chunky, high spirited, good-natured woman. His Dad passed away several years ago, followed by his mom about 10 years later. It was tough saying goodbye to both of them. The loss of both of his parents left John-O in a bit of a state of loneliness. He had one brother, but their relationship was rocky since the passing of their mother.

After many years of running around together, including John participating as a groomsman in our wedding, there was a time when there was some distance. I remember John and Spencer hanging out in Freeport at the Nautical Mile once and, at the time, we only had one car so I called Spencer to come pick me up at the train station when I got in from work from New York City. This call interrupted their time at the Mile and John was not happy about it. When they came to pick me up, they were all a little tipsy and John and I exchanged some words to the point that he called me a Bitch. I was shocked and a little devastated, had no intention of fighting with him. I told Spencer to drop me off and they could carry on their night, but it was impossible to do this since Spencer was also concerned about our exchange of words. For a while after this, there was some tension in the friendship. I personally didn't speak to John for some time, but then years later when Spencer's sister Brooke passed away, John came back around by expressing his condolences and it was like nothing about the friendship had ever changed. We were also touched by a note he wrote to us in thanks for the condolences on the loss of his mom, and from there we moved on with our friendship without looking back.

We officially opened a gourmet restaurant on Long Beach Road in Oceanside on my birthday on 10/10/14. I told you, crazy things happen on my birthday. It was called Cheffy's Corner Cuisine. It was Spencer's lifelong dream to open a restaurant so, believing in his skills, expertise and passion for food, we used all of our savings to fund his dream.

Then that awful night came. One night before closing the restaurant, I had made plans to go to a comedy club in Manhattan with my girlfriend for her birthday. I was somewhat hesitant to go because Spencer would be closing the restaurant alone, but I ignored my gut and left him there to close anyway. That night Spencer got a call from

John to meet him at the Smith Street park event that guys from the neighborhood had hosted there for the past three years or so. We went there briefly the year before and Spencer had said he wouldn't go back since he didn't want to be in an area where any conflict could be caused and this area was known for that based on riffs of the past he may have been involved in.

Back in high school, this particular area of Uniondale, the south side was the other side of town from where we lived in Uniondale on the North so there was always a hint of beef analogous to the East Coast - West Coast rap beef of Biggie and Tupac. Against his better judgment, he answered John's call and went to meet him out at the park by himself. When I spoke to him around 9, he said he was heading out from the restaurant to go there. Once he got there, Spencer connected with John and a few others he knew from his high school days.

Spencer was speaking to John casually when out of nowhere a dude with short dreads started to come towards Spencer yelling at him and attempting to get up in his face. Spencer had no idea who it was and he backed up and began his natural response which is to throw up his hands to protect himself. The person said things in Spencer's face like " I went to war for you back in the day" as if to say he'd done so much for Spencer and now he was reliving some sort of old grief and hard times he was remembering randomly. Someone on the side said "Doug, chill!" and attempted to pull him back and at that point

Spencer realized who it was. It was Doug Kramer. Doug was also once a friend in our circle in high school but after an argument in Dutch's basement twenty years before where they exchanged words and had a shoving match, we had not ever seen him again. That night alcohol was involved, and this night it was also.

Spencer had just got to the park, so thankfully he had not been drinking, but apparently Doug had been there at the park drinking most of the day and his words and actions reflected his intention to want to fight. Once Spencer realized Doug was calling him out to fight, he got angry and wanted to get out of the park immediately, away from all the extra spectators. He lured Doug out of the park to go somewhere down the block to square off away from all the others. As he started to leave and get in his car, Doug followed him. John-O ran off with Spencer and tried to calm him down. All along Spencer was asking John why he brought him out there knowing this dude was in the park and they didn't get along. John said chill, we are going to handle this, and we are going to work it out. But at this point the tensions were too high and it was a race to get down the block. As both cars took off down the block violently, Christian, a friend of all the guys since high school, was also on the block at the time following in his own car. As all three cars approached the block of Turtle Hook, something like a spirit came over Spencer and he decided he was going to leave the scene and drop this nonsense. As Spencer saw Doug park and pull over and start walking hurriedly and angrily over towards his car, Spencer made the decision to leave. John-O was happy to know that Spencer was backing down so he got out of the car to go talk to Doug and John-O said his good-byes to Spencer.

While Doug approached John, Spencer sped off angrily and called me immediately and told me what had just happened. He said, "Babe, these niggas are trying to play me!" I could barely understand him and asked him to calm down and tell me what was going on. He told me the whole story and I thanked God he left the scene and told him he did the right thing and that I was so proud of him. The old Spencer would have certainly stayed and escalated the conflict into a physical altercation. He still considered going back after him. I could hear how pumped his adrenaline was and how angry he was that he was in this position. I am sure he wished he had never gone out there at all from the beginning. I begged him to go home and try to stay calm and to go to bed and he said that he would. I told him I would be home as soon as I could and we hung up. I was able to confirm a little bit later from my son Max that he did go home and was fast asleep in bed. He turned off his phone and didn't even answer my later calls to him. I ended up leaving the comedy show early and headed home, reaching home about midnight. I was happy to know he was fast asleep in bed.

Early the next morning, I woke up to a Facebook messenger post from Dutch's sister at 5:08 am on 7/19/15 that said: "GM, tell Spencer John-O is in the Hospital…Urgent, my brother is there now, Bad!!!!

He's unconscious." Once I told Spencer this he jumped up and turned on his phone to a barrage of messages from several people that had heard about what happened after Spencer left. It turns out that John-O came into contact with Doug, attempting to calm him down and talk him off his explosive rage, and instead of Doug responding appropriately and calming down, he turned his anger on John-O and started cursing him out and remarking about issues he had with him in the past related to his old girlfriend and that John-O was responsible for them breaking up. Out of nowhere he sucker punched John-O in the side of his head. It was so bad that John-O collapsed onto the sidewalk unconscious and bleeding from his head. Luckily Christian was there and assumedly contacted an ambulance which took John-O to the hospital.

We arrived at the Nassau University Medical Center hospital as quickly as we could. When we arrived there were several people in the waiting area as well at John's bedside. Their faces were all solemn, serious, unsmiling and grave. Spencer was devastated at the appearance of seeing John in the bed. He was broken and in shock and rightly so. John was unconscious, not moving, his head all wrapped up and he was clearly in bad shape with blood spots showing on his wounds. The doctors said he had lost a lot of blood, but they were working on him and over a day or so thought the prognosis could not necessarily be determined, but was slowly turning for the better. This changed quickly. A day or so later John's condition took a turn for the worse. The bleeding wouldn't stop and eventually the doctors pronounced him brain dead.

It was only a matter of time now that his family, now only his brother since both his parents were dead, had to make a decision to turn off his ventilator. This was very complicated for all of us since we knew John and his brother were not speaking at this time. Since his mother died, they'd fought over many things, including her will and other material items. He and his brother had not been getting along at all, and now he was charged with making the decision to pull the plug on John's life which he did.

John officially passed away on July 30th 2015. His funeral took place about a week later on August 8th. It was very difficult for us all to say goodbye. In his casket he did not even look like himself. He looked just like his brother instead. The two always had a keen resemblance. This time it was eerie. I was asked to read a passage from the Bible for his service. I was very nervous, but knew I had to do this for our friend, our brother. We all hesitantly said our final goodbyes and gathered outside to see his casket driven off in the hearse. We found out a few months later that he was cremated and his remains still had not been picked up from the funeral home. John was having some difficulties communicating with his children, especially his son's Mom at the time of his death. Spencer had been in touch with his brother for a little while, but slowly the communication stopped. This experience left a very deep hole in Spencer's heart.

He'd loved John for many years and in many ways he was like a brother to him.

I wrote this post on Facebook the day before his funeral that summed up what I was feeling about him…

Dear John,

As we prepare to celebrate you going home to the Promised Land, let me say this, you were one of the funniest and coolest guys I know! A sensitive Pisces, born on March 13th, we celebrated your birthday and many other family events with you by our side. You were at our side for our wedding day, the formal dinner at Brasserie with my stepfather JC, in my backyard for countless BBQ'S practically every weekend, and of course the life of the party at the non-baby shower for my cousin where you made it clear you would not play any of the "games" but jumped into every single one (especially Hip Hop Charades) like the winner and hip hop king that you are! None of what happened to you makes sense to any of us who love you, but ultimately we know the truth and wish none of this ever happened. Once upon a time we had our own personal little riff and at the end of the day, you told me you loved me, I was your sister and always family to you and even in the midst of the distance, I always believed that. My husband has loved you and called you his best friend his whole life, which made it no choice for me to love you as well. I watched you have and love your beautiful daughter with my old friend and play basketball with your handsome son like true Ballers! You even challenged teenagers on the court and schooled my friend's kids in the Art of the game. I even helped you get your b-ball coaching business live and on LinkedIn! You named all my kids with outrageous nicknames like Ah-lan-B(Princess), JoBanna (JV) and that Wild Kid from NeBraska (Max)... all with strong emphasis on the BBBBB's!! When you came through, it was absolutely going to be a blast even if you ended up on my couch over night, I was happy knowing that you were safe. Well...you are certainly safe now! Please don't get mad at all your pictures I posted on Facebook (I know you hate social media) but know that I love you, always did and always will!!!! RIP my brother... Yours Truly

P.S. I don't want to cry anymore, I want to celebrate you...I AM A BELIEVER. Kiss your sweet Mom and Dad for me. #DoDamagePossie4Life

Gia

More recently, in 2017, I lost two other good friends approximately one week apart. The first loss was my girl Gia Williams on Dec. 20, 2017 and the second was Dylan who for many years was like a brother to me, gone on December 27, 2017. These were both two young people in my eyes, the same age as me, 49 and 48 respectively and their deaths were not only shocking, but untimely.

Gia was an old high school classmate. We got together a few times then, but we grew closest during the past seven years. I ran into Gia again after many years at one of the Possie BBQ's that my best friend Nick throws with his boys every year. About 40 of the fellas all collect money and come together to host a large family event in the park complete with food, music and t-shirts displaying a slogan or message that fulfills the dream theme of the year. That year Gia came with her other girlfriends and she and I spent a little while talking. She was down on herself about her weight and made some comments that revealed her self-esteem was very low. I remember distinctly at that moment reminding her of what a beautiful person she was inside and out and she should never forget that. From that moment on we became fast friends and spent lots of time coming together for various social gatherings. Whenever I had a get together, I invited her over.

The week before she died, she and I talked about her coming over to my house for Christmas. I had planned a brunch with lots of champagne and lots of food. I usually always spend Christmas at my mother-in-law's house, but this year I wanted to stay home. Gia promised to bring her famous deviled eggs and some pulled pork and she talked about the recovery of her mom who had fallen down the steps at her house sometime before Thanksgiving. She was terribly worried about her and after going in and out of the hospital she promised she would come over for the holiday but not stay long since she would also be spending time with her mom. Gia had her own health problems. She was currently wearing a vest that she was supposed to have on all the time to check her heart rate because she was having trouble with it which was complicating the MS she had been dealing with for years.

Gia never made it over for Christmas. The week before Christmas I received word from a friend that she had been found in her home dead from heart failure. I was getting off the train when I got the call and immediately broke down in tears. Gia was having trouble wearing the heart monitor. She was annoyed by the look of it, and felt it was a task to wear it so often went without it. She recently confided in me about the marital problems she was having with her husband who she barely knew. He was an African Uber driver and she took a chance on marrying him so he could get his citizenship papers, but found out quickly that he was a womanizer and not as supportive and loving to her as she thought he should be. She also expressed that her closest friends did not support the marriage and were distancing themselves from her. She spent some days crying to me and I offered her as much support as I could. I told Spencer the last time she cried to me right before Christmas that she did not sound good at all and that I was worried about her. It was so bad between her and her husband that at one point rumors circulated about possible foul play involved and that maybe he was responsible for her death.

That theory was eventually squashed. It would have been too much to take.

Gia's mom was devastated about losing her. I went to see her to offer my condolences and support. She was so devastated that she didn't have a memorial or a service for her that I know of. Gia had also confided in me that she was not feeling supported from many of her friends. I believed she was torn between her friends and her new husband. As she spoke to me I knew she had been drinking. Shortly before that, in the summer, I met her at a friend's house out east and she had too much to drink that day as well. She became very belligerent and argumentative with her friend and it was clear that it was time for her to call it a night. My daughter had to drive her car home. Spencer and I followed behind her when Princess drove her home.

We had a repeat event one night later in the summer at the Nautical Mile where she had too much to drink and I had to lift her to get her into the car after she fell down on the street. She was heavier than the amount of weight I could carry. Luckily, a few people who were out partying on their way to the restaurant saw me struggling with her in front of Tropix and were kind enough to help me lift her into the car. I was so worried for her. I made her come home with me and I would not let her leave. I held her keys and begged her to stay and she finally agreed. She slept on the couch and left the next morning. After she'd recuperated she called and thanked me for the love. I never judged her because we have all been there at one time or another; you just hope it is not too late before you realize you have had one too many drinks.

Dylan

A week after Gia's death, I received the devastating news of the loss of my old friend Dylan who was like a brother to me. Dylan is the father of my goddaughter Paige and the ex-boyfriend of my friend Stella. Stella was a friend to me throughout high school. We went away to college together where we ended up being roommates and eventually housemates together. When we moved back home from college she spent some time living at my house with me in Uniondale after leaving her apartment in Hempstead. Her mom asked me if it was okay for her to come and live with me and of course I said yes since that's what friends are for. Dylan and Stella had dated since high school and into college on and off until they had Paige. Not long after they ended up breaking up because Dylan also had another relationship with a woman who he lived a mirror life with. He bought her the same gifts he bought Stella. He took her to the same places he took Stella. In the end, both girls had babies for Dylan just one month apart. It was around this time that they found out about each other. In the end, Stella left Dylan and he ended up staying with his other girlfriend and actually marrying her. Paige and Dylan's son Zee grew up together and have remained close which is comforting to see which I know would make him proud.

What I knew about Dylan for a while is that he had problems with his pancreas. Pancreatic issues tend to be connected to alcohol use and although Dylan was not supposed to be drinking alcohol, he did anyway. Dylan was a party guy. He enjoyed house music, getting dressed up nice and going out late into the night for a good vibe. He almost always had CJ with him who we all saw as his partner in crime. Where there was Dylan, there was CJ. One such night was our 30th year high school reunion in the summer of 2017. Dylan had hit me up asking where the festivities were happening that weekend for our reunion and before long, he showed up at the Nautical Mile where about 15 of us were hanging out. We laughed so much about old jokes, old teachers and great memories. We didn't want the party to end so I brought everyone over to my house for the after party. We continued talking and joking around while listening to music. That night Dylan and I were talking and at one point, while he was sipping on a drink, he leaned over to me and said, "You know you are my sister, right?" and I looked him right in his eye and said, "Yes Dylan, and you are my brother and always will be." That moment was surreal as I think back on it now, not knowing that in less than six months he would be gone.

Dylan ended up in the hospital unexpectedly. There were some complications and we received word from other good friends that

Dylan was gone. I couldn't believe it. This was a very difficult way to end the year. His funeral was in early January at my church, the Queen of the Most Holy Rosary. He and his parents were members there. This made it all the more surreal, but definitely more comforting to see my priest Father Joseph eulogize Dylan and send him home well. After the funeral and burial at the Greenfield Cemetery in Uniondale, we all went to the repast at a hall in Roosevelt. There was a collage of pictures running on the screen once we arrived and got settled. Seeing all the pictures with him and his family and me and our friends was hard to take.

Spencer prepared some food we offered to bring and at the end of the day, I was overwhelmed with grief. I helped serve the food since I thought it was the least I could do to help. Still, it didn't feel like enough. I remember one time the following summer after Dylan died, while we were all hanging out in Olivia and Nick's backyard preparing to watch Power, I said, "What's up with Dylan, is he coming?" I caught myself at the last second as the words came out of my mouth and everyone just looked at me with no expression. I forgot for one brief moment that he was no longer with us. Dylan let me drive his car in high school when I was learning to drive (before I got my license), and he always made sure I was protected and taken care of when we all hung out. He really treated me like his little sister. These memories, I will never forget.

Josie

When 2018 arrived I started to feel very worried and anxious about the recent losses that had occurred with friends that were all my age. Not long after this, my sister-in-law Josie had an episode at home that appeared to resemble a stroke. She was unable to talk, so Spencer's sister, June, called an ambulance and got her to the hospital. Spencer, Princess and I met them there. Once there, the doctors were concerned that they could not get her to respond verbally and decided it was necessary to intubate her if we agreed to find out exactly what was going on. This is something Josie never really wanted. She always said that if she was going to die, let her die, but at this point we were not sure this was the case and the hope always was to do what we could to save her or at least find out what was happening. Spencer spoke to his mother and June and they all went ahead and made the decision to intubate her. Intubating her involved inserting a tube into her trachea in order to restore her own breathing although artificially.

We stayed outside the room while they did the procedure and we could hear her discomfort with this process. Once they stabilized her, we were able to come back into the room. The neurologist came and gave her an assessment. When we told the doctor what was wrong with her and the diagnosis of Fred Reich's ataxia, he immediately told us this was not that. He said her behaviors and abilities did not suggest that disease at all. He could not immediately figure out what was going on, but after staying in the hospital a few nights the reports did confirm she had a stroke. She had also been experiencing seizures, which is what seemingly brought her to the hospital on that night in the first place.

She was in the hospital for almost two weeks with the doctors trying to figure out her case and what they could do for her. After a while we made a decision to remove the intubation and take our chances on what would happen to her because we knew and could see that she was uncomfortable and would not want this. The doctor was worried that without the intubation she would certainly die shortly thereafter, but he was wrong. They removed the tubes and kept her on oxygen as a precautionary measure and she did fine, though her eating and breathing habits changed and went up and down periodically. She was improving enough to be moved. We knew she wanted to be home and my mother-in-law was also adamant that they bring her home so we made preparations to bring her home into hospice care at the doctor's recommendation since there was nothing more they could do for her in the hospital.

We finally got her transported home on a Sunday. It was so comforting to know that she was back home in her own bed. A medical bed was in place that helped her move up and down and was useful in cleaning and feeding her, which my mother-in-law had to do every day with the help of June and the girls. Eventually, they started giving her morphine since she seemed to be in pain from what appeared to be painful expressions on her face. Everyone knew she was slowly deteriorating. She didn't talk at all in the hospital or when she came home, but eventually she started to make better eye contact and much later on started to mouth and whisper certain words. At one point we even thought she looked like she was getting better, but in between that time she may have had more seizures and the stress was taking a toll on her body.

My daughter JV was about to get married in the month of April, but Josie was too sick to attend the wedding. JV tried on her dress for her and also came by to see her the morning of the wedding with her hair done so she could see her. Josie's face lit up so bright when she saw JV with her Cinderella "up-do". She told JV she loved her and we all just cried with tears of joy.

Less than a month later my mother-in-law recognized that Josie was giving up the fight. For a few days she would not eat at all. Mary had created many healthy food choices to give Josie her strength, things like Nutriment and a clear liquid drink called Arrowroot which was a Caribbean remedy that after a while Josie just refused to take. She would tighten her lips when it was brought to her mouth in the syringe and at that point Mary knew it was only a matter of time. For the next few days we were at Josie's bedside almost 24/7.

The day before Josie's death a nurse came and advised us that the signs of death had started. She was sleeping most of the time, her breathing was sporadic, and when her eyes were open, they were not moving at all. On the last day it was surreal how the day played out. We stayed near her bed the entire day, praying. At one point Mary was so confused she didn't know what to do. I suggested we pray the rosary and she agreed. The entire family sat around Josie's bed praying the rosary and, for some reason, this moment brought such utter and complete calm to the situation. A few of us decided to leave the house and go pick up food for everyone; Princess, Max, Sydney and I left together. While we were out, we received word that Josie had taken her last breath on 5/5/2018. Spencer, June, my mother and Mary were present at the time to experience Josie's transformation from this world to the next.

When we got back, we could see her peaceful body at rest. Everyone was just moving around in strange harmony, waiting for the hospice nurse to come and make the pronouncement of death. When the nurse finally arrived about three hours later, Josie's death now seemed final. Spencer contacted the funeral home since he had already made previous arrangements and not long afterward they came and prepared her body for departure. Once again, as with Brooke, watching the funeral home take Josie's body bag out of the house was more than some of us could bear. June literally lost it and suddenly had an asthma attack. Everyone was working to get her to calm down because we did not need her to be sick in that moment with what was already happening in the house. We were extremely worried about her.

Spencer and I followed Josie's body outside to the truck the funeral home came in. As we walked outside and watched them put her body in the truck and close the door, at that same moment a church chime from the Methodist Church down the block started ringing. It was 9:00 pm, so it rang nine bells. The timing was so perfect that Spencer and I looked at each other with divine faith. We knew God had her and that he was watching over her now. Even if that bell rang every other night at 9:00, this was the only night we ever heard it. The sound brought a feeling of comfort to our souls.

Josie was cremated within the next week and the funeral home delivered her ashes to the house. June had already picked out a beautiful urn and Mary was happy to receive her. We established her memorial service for the following week and it turned out to be a beautiful service. All of the children participated and we gathered as a family in the church hall following the memorial. It was a long day. Right after Josie's memorial mass, I went back to church to be the lector for that Saturday's 5:30 mass. Not sure how it turned out that way, but I didn't complain. I enjoyed the time I gave reading the word. While everyone stayed at the house and socialized, I left for church again and came back home content from the day. It is well with my soul. It is well, it is well, with my soul.

12

History Repeats Itself

After living such a difficult life of guilt for the decisions I had made with abortion and many other things, I constantly counseled both my daughters, but especially JV, on the importance of loving relationships and birth control and/or abstinence until the time was right. Like most children, my coaching went from one ear right through the other. She was taken to the OBGYN and prescribed birth control, but possibly did not take heed to my advice.

JV and I had a very rocky relationship for a period of time. I made the assumption that it was based on her feelings of disconnect in being the one child who was not my husband Spencer's child. She'd had a hard time with this for most of her young life. All four of our other children had Spencer for their father, but she had a different father, Wayne, who was participating in her life. I can understand this feeling of exclusion in her mind. However, I spent a great deal of time as a parent trying to ensure she and all of the kids felt connected to us similarly since we were a blended family. With that said, it still made her feel different. As much as I would like to think so, and believe I could control her feelings, it's clear that I could not change something she felt. It is difficult for me to believe that I could not protect her and make her feel included. At times I wanted to correct her feelings, but it's not easy to change how someone else is feeling. It's their feeling and theirs alone. I could only continue to guide her, let her know I loved her and offer her support when she was challenged with life's tough decisions.

I wasn't sure JV would make it out of high school based on a few episodes she had of bad judgment. There was a period of time in junior high school that she ran away from home after having a huge verbal disagreement with Spencer during which I was sure he was going to physically beat her. It was Thanksgiving Day. We had sat down to eat and she started to say something smart and disrespectful to him and that's when it got heated between them. She said something like the typical "You're not my father; don't tell me what to do." Then she literally ran out of the house. Spencer said he was going to call her father because he was about to light her up and beat her ass for the disrespect she was throwing out at him.

We couldn't find her for a few days. We searched everywhere, called all of her friends and started to get worried. Wayne was even looking for her in the Bronx since we got a hint that she may be out there which was not entirely true. Eventually, I received word that she was with some friends who I didn't care for very much and we talked her into coming back home. The morning I went to meet her to talk to her and take her to school, or so she thought, Spencer and I picked her up and instead took her to the airport. JV was going to be on the next plane to Jamaica, West Indies. It appeared she was shocked and upset, but the look in her eyes also told me that she was okay with this decision and ready to start a new chapter in her life. She knew what she was getting into.

JV and her sister had spent many summers in Jamaica with my Mom and JC who had moved back there after retirement. I was so worried about leaving her alone at home EVER again after the scare she gave me by running away that I made the decision to send her to live with my mother in Jamaica for a little while. Even though she cried, I think at 15, a part of her was ready to re-group and start over again. This was one of the toughest decisions I ever had to make in my life. At this point I don't regret it, but I was worried that the streets and bad company were going to take her away from me forever.

After taking her to the airport I went home to Freeport where we lived at the time, got in bed and cried for hours. I was not able to calm down until I knew she had made it into my mother's arms. I had my own fear of flying at this time, so the combination of making the decision to put her on the plane by herself that day along with wondering if I was doing the right thing placed a heavy feeling of fear on my heart. If anything happened to her I would never be able to forgive myself. Once my mother received her in Jamaica, I was only slightly calmer. The next few weeks I focused on working with my mom to get her settled in.

She was home schooled for a short period and then eventually attended a school in Jamaica that my mother set her up in. She got a job in a local fabric store with a friend of my mothers. After a while she started to adapt and make friends, and even seemed to be enjoying it there. JV spent about a year in Jamaica. She turned 16 there, and that summer I went to pick her up and bring her back home. By then we had moved from the house in Freeport so I could get her away from the crowd she was running with at the time. I also had Max and we knew we could use more space for the kids.

We bought a bigger house in the Harbor. Everyone had their own room and when she came home to the new house she seemed very happy and began to grow up in front of our eyes very quickly. Eventually she started dating here and there and ultimately ended up dating a guy who, for whatever reason, did not connect with my spirit very well at all.

She made it through high school and eventually went to Adelphi University. It wasn't my first choice for her to go to school because it was very expensive, almost three times the cost of a state school because it was private. Old Westbury, the school I graduated from with my Bachelor's in Sociology, was my first choice for her but she didn't want to go there. I helped her with student loans and after the first semester on campus, she decided to quit and come back home. I was a little hurt and disappointed that she didn't finish, and it was a super expensive lesson for me as I was carrying student loans on her behalf on my credit.

At one point in January, JV told me she was considering an online program. She said she wanted to get her healthcare degree through Red Lobster where she was working at the time. She opened a savings account and was trying to do some things on her own. Two weeks later I heard through Spencer's nephew that while dating this guy named Morgan, my biggest fear for her happened...she ended up pregnant. By the time I found out, she was 11 weeks along.

JV felt like I had changed in my relationship with Spencer, and I did change. I was not an independent single mother, I was married. She thought I was always trying to please Spencer even when, to her, it seemed he wasn't treating me right. We have had our problems with Spencer's excessive drinking at times and I ending up going through a depression as a result of us both over drinking, spending very little time at home, and taking risks that almost broke up our marriage. There was a time when we spent a lot of time out drinking, getting into trouble with so called friends and not working on the things that should have been more important to us at the time, like taking care of our children, our home and our finances. As I tried to explain to JV, there is a lot of give and take in relationships. I told her that one day when she was married she would understand. I see how she is different when she is with her boyfriend. It shows me that she is a family-oriented person. She hated Spencer's controlling temperament, mindset and behavior, and I did too. However, we were still growing as a couple.

One day during her pregnancy, when I was at a PTA meeting, JV and Spencer got into a huge argument. It was one of the many that took place in the house. They were talking, and her tone with him was very nonchalant and rude. She boldly said she was not doing certain chores around the house and pretty much dared him to have a problem with it. Long story short, the argument didn't end well and he told her he wanted her out of the house. He said she had to find somewhere else to live within the next two weeks. I told him that this was ridiculous and even though it may be apparent that they couldn't live together, he couldn't expect her to find somewhere to live in two weeks. He stomped around the house for about a week because he was angry and we were not communicating about this at all. I told them both what a fucked up position they were putting me in yet neither one seemed to care. They were both just thinking of themselves.

When it didn't seem as if something was going to come through for JV for an apartment, Spencer packed some things and decided to go stay at his mother's house for a few days. He says because he was so angry about JV he did not want to be around and risk there would be another incident with him and his temper. This is one of the things I have struggled with for some time about my husband. He has the worst temper ever! He ended up going to stay at his Mom's house less than two miles down the road. He was gone almost three weeks and we fought on and off about the whole thing. One weekend we decided to get away by going into the city to take a break from it all. It was a really tough time. The trip helped a bit since we were both able to talk about the situation and come to some agreements.

In February of that year, JV moved into her own place. She found a room across the street from where her boyfriend Morgan's house was. It was his best friend's house. It wasn't the best place, but it wasn't the worst, either. Morgan's best friend lived there with his Dad and a tenant rented another room. It felt a little bittersweet helping her get settled in. It reminded me a little of the small apartment Wayne and I shared in North Carolina when I was pregnant with her. There had been two other renters in the house and we literally had one small room.

In essence I believed it was time for JV to move on. She was about to have a baby of her own and was starting to build and create a life for herself. I knew it would be tough for her, but she would figure it out. Over time it would all work out…in God's time. On March 30th of that year, JV found out she was having a boy. She did the best she could getting used to living on her own. She called me every day asking about cooking, filing taxes, and plenty more! She talked to me more now that she was on her own than she ever did.

On Memorial Day weekend JV went into pre-term labor and was having contractions on and off the whole weekend. She wasn't due until August. Right now the baby was 3lbs and 5ozs. She went into the hospital at 1 am and I got there at 3 am. The contractions were coming, but eventually stopped. So she would have to stay in the hospital until the doctor gave us further notice. I was hoping to try and find her another apartment in the coming weeks since she really needed her own space for when the baby came. She had decided on a name for him, JC as a nickname, after her grandpa who she was closest to.

Her friend and I had been talking about planning a baby shower for JV. It was all really crazy how history was repeating itself. The same thing happened to me on June 26, 1989. JV was born at 3lbs. 6ozs! What a surprise that she turned out to be a girl, the whole time she was in my stomach I thought she was a boy. I was in the hospital for one month having the same pre-term labor symptoms she was experiencing now, but worse. I had dilated two centimeters already and had to stay on bed rest for the next month. JV was born on July 26, 1989 and came home on August 26, 1989. I had her at 31weeks, and right now JV was 27 weeks pregnant. .

JV was lucky enough to make it through the pre-term labor scare. It turned out she was just a bit dehydrated, received some fluid and was then released from the hospital. From that point on we all assumed the baby would come early. By now she was four days past her due date and my life was up in the air. I didn't go on our July 4th family vacation we planned to Florida to visit my Dad because I couldn't leave her and risk that she would go into labor. It was my sincere desire to be present for her in the delivery room. We had her baby shower on June 20th. We rushed it thinking she wouldn't make it to the original planned shower date in July. Now, on August 13th her mucus plug broke. We are getting closer and closer to the delivery date.

All the emotions that came with this process are so strange. How can someone feel so many emotions at the same time? I was disappointed for her because I knew it is so hard being a sort of single parent. Although she had a boyfriend, it's just not the same since I didn't get the feeling that he was very supportive. I was worried for her. I was sad that she and Spencer didn't have a close relationship. I was excited to be become a grandmother, anticipating little JC and who he would look like, hoping that she got a bigger apartment and praying that her and Morgan do their best to grow into their relationship together.

It is interesting that not that long ago, maybe 1-2 years, I asked Spencer if we could have another baby. I was 38. He point blank told me we had enough kids and that it just wouldn't make sense. I knew deep down inside he was right, but I just felt like my biological clock was ticking and memories of being pregnant and feeling like a child and that I could no longer be a child-bearing woman were plaguing me. I was feeling like soon my body would no longer be able to make babies so I just got worried and sort of depressed. Shortly thereafter is when I found out JV was pregnant. What a crazy feeling. I felt my young life coming back to see me again and leaving all at the same time, with no regrets.

JV called me at 5am on August 14th to tell me she was on her way to the hospital. Her friend Michelle was taking her there. She woke up that morning to a bit of blood in her bed. When I heard this I immediately became concerned but told her it was okay and that everything was going to be fine. I got to the hospital at 5:45 am but not before updating my Facebook status to say "This is it!" I was ready to meet my first grandson.

What I thought was moving right along nearly halted. Her contractions slowed down halfway through the process. She was experiencing a great deal of pain. I tried to encourage her to go pain killer free, but by 8 pm she couldn't handle the pain anymore. The whole family came up to see her at about 9 pm including Spencer, which truly was a surprise. Princess and her two friends came to visit her also. She was so funny looking because she was sitting up in the bed like a genie in a bottle trying to find a comfortable position to stay in. She looked like she was meditating during the whole labor process. In the end she really handled it well. She started pushing at approximately 2:45 am almost 24 hours later. At about 3:15 am, Morgan and I went with her into the actual delivery room. After pushing for another 30 minutes her beautiful son Josiah Kordell Overton was born. He was 7 lbs. 4 oz. and 20 and three-quarter inches long. They took him away quickly because while JV was in labor she had a fever of 101.9. They weren't sure if the baby may have also caught an infection so they were being cautious. While he was in the hospital, only the parents and grandparents could see him. He was so well-behaved for the three days he was in the hospital. I was in awe of his little face.

After he went home I went to see him every day. I'm so overwhelmed by the concept of being a grandmother, he is just so cute! He looks just like Max when he was born. I hope they grow to look like and be great friends. Later on that week, I wrote JV a letter that said...

Dear JV,

My first born... Let me start by saying congratulations on experiencing the most wonderful feeling God himself has to offer. Creating a life by HIS WILL and bringing your son into this world to endure all life has to offer; happiness, disappointment, desire, shame, love, and pain; all of this will come, because this is what life is all about. I am proud of you for making a decision to keep your child growing inside of you and not deciding to abort him or give him up for adoption to another well-deserving family. This is the decision of a lifetime and I'm pleased with the decision you made. As I said from day one, it is not going to be easy, but no matter what, I will be there for you when you need me. That is what I promised myself when I gave birth to you 20 years ago. This is the promise I will keep forever. Although it will be difficult at times you must always challenge yourself to do your best and to strive to get ahead of the game. There are many ways to get ahead of the game; staying in school, saving money, not spending frivolously, staying in church or prayerful, not gossiping, working hard, treating people with respect and all the other important things that you would want for yourself. Your son is my first grandson and that is very special. I am now going to have no choice but to worry about him as much as I worry about you. In his first few weeks of life you have to ensure that he is protected from those things that can harm him, like bacteria, too many people in his space, and the like. Please be aware of this and do your best to manage your surroundings accordingly. I know you will do the right thing because I can see and feel the love you have for him from a mile away. I will try to maintain my personal feelings and allow you your space to grow and raise him your way. I encourage you to ask for my advice and to listen to those around you that you respect and know have the experience of parenting. I had no idea I would feel this overwhelmed by the joy Josiah brings to our family. Many times I've wished you were still living with me and then I pray that you keep your independent mind and do better for yourself and your family as time goes on. I feel like this is the way you will be able to do that. Following in my footsteps almost exactly overwhelms me with joy and pain because it reminds me of all the difficult things I have been through. These difficulties made me a stronger and smarter person, taught me to turn the other cheek, to wish the best for others, to want harmony in life and to look at myself in the mirror daily and know that I am a good person. I know you are a good person also. I wish you all the blessings life has to offer you and your new family. I will pray for you all dearly and look forward to all the future special times we will be together. I love you and again... Congratulations.

JV wrote me back and said...

Mom,

I read your email the day you told me that you sent it to me and I just got emotional reading it so it took some time to respond. I know it was a big disappointment to hear that I was pregnant and I'm so grateful that you decided to help me instead of disowning me like you somewhat experienced from your father. You were right about this being hard, because even in the early stages I was such a nervous wreck that everything seemed worse than it was. I'm glad you are concerned about protecting Josiah as well. That's how grandmothers are supposed to be. I want you to participate as much as you'd like to. Josiah is just as much yours as he is mine. After all, I am still learning how to be a mother, and I can say I'm learning from the best. You are such an inspiration to me and I've seen you go through hell and back. Part of the trials and tribulations you faced were because of me, and now that I've seen at least the beginning of what you've done for me, I can truly say I AM SORRY. You've given me all of the opportunities in the world and even though there were times when I didn't seem as though I was grateful, I want you to know that I was, and I will always be grateful. You are the most important person in my life and even though Jojo and Morgan are around and I am forming my own family, you are still the one I need the most. You believe in me and now I realize that everything you have done for me you have done for a reason, and I thank you so much. I love you and can't wait to walk down this path with your support and guidance. Love always, "your favorite" - Dova

In the short term, I found out Morgan was being abusive to JV. When we found out, Spencer, Wayne and I put our heads together on how we were going to handle it. There was a time we were trying to track him down and were alerted to the fact that he had moved away from his mother and grandmother's house and never came back to see Josiah again since he was a year old.

JV ended up dating again and creating a new love bond with a great guy by the name of Cyprian who she knew for many years through her connections in Uniondale. They eventually grew to form a wonderful, loving relationship and JV moved in with Cyprian and his family in Uniondale. Cyprian's family reminds me very much of my Spencer and his family. His grandmother is a devout Catholic, just like Mary. He has a sister who he is very close with, like Spencer is with his sisters and they all live together in one house with his Mom and her husband. They welcomed JV into their family with loving arms and I am very appreciative of that every day.

After seven years of being together, Cyprian and JV began discussing marriage. They slipped questions in about it here and there, not very directly, since I am sure they didn't want the pressure. At first it was JV more so than Cyprian. In my opinion it's typical that the woman is the one who is more interested in settling down whereas the man may be more inclined to wait. I don't know about their personal conversations together and who said what, but it came to a point that they were talking about it seriously. Cyprian eventually went to the Bronx and talked to Wayne about his interest in marrying JV. He also discussed it with us, and of course we said we would support whatever they wanted to do.

It took them about a year to finally get truly serious about moving forward with the plan to get married and then a date was set! They chose April 20, 2018 which is coincidentally the same day as the Great American smoke out for all you weed smokers out there. Why they chose that day I don't know, but that is what they settled on. Once the date was selected, the planning craze was underway.

I give JV a lot of credit. Like me when I planned my wedding, I had a vision of how I wanted it all to take place and did it all on my own. She prepared all of her ideas, created a huge binder of materials with every idea in it like I am sure most women do when they are planning a wedding. She asked me questions here and there, but she immediately knew they wanted Spencer and Upscale International Caterers to do the food for the wedding, which we would not have had any other way. Spencer had left his full-time job to be an entrepreneur which he has been at heart for many years. He and his team created a high-end catering and meal plan business about a year before JV's wedding that they offered to the tri-state area. They'd had great success with it.

Once all the planning came down to the fast approaching deadline of 4/20, the finances got a little haywire. JV's budget went a little beyond what she had initially planned, so luckily we were able to help her out a lot. Spencer had already agreed to cater the wedding at no cost so that was a huge help. The only thing they had to do was pay for the labor to cover the costs of the staff. In addition, we bought the flowers and helped her out with a few things as needed. Her father and Bailey helped her out as well. Still, with all the planning happening, I was worried that JV still hadn't received an engagement ring. Cyprian had some ideas of ring options and eventually sent me a picture of the actual ring, but no action had taken place to give it to her yet. He knew me and her sister Princess wanted to be involved with the moment he actually proposed.

Finally, at the 12th hour, he came up with his own plan. He decided to take her into the city in Central Park for a horse and carriage ride. When they got to a part of the park where the horses park, they walked over the bridge to a lit area in the park and he was about to propose to her. Princess and I were there the whole time, stalking them, and JV had no idea. We followed along with them in a bicycle cart but stayed stealth the whole time. We came up on them at the time Cyprian got down on bended knee and we got it all on videotape. We were so happy to have watched that moment for them. Afterwards, we all met back at the head of the park and congratulated them on what an exciting moment this was.

Before long the time had come. The day of my daughter's wedding to her soul mate, the love of her life had come. We had a lot of family in town at the time. My mom came home early from Jamaica, Grandma Gemma came from Florida, my sister Victoria from Florida, and my Aunt Lola was here from Atlanta, and all my close friends from high school. The night before the wedding we had the wedding rehearsal at my house. The entire bridal party showed up. They took their time to follow through on the plan and everyone played their part for the event. JV had all her sisters and brothers in the wedding except Wayne's other daughter Amanda. Amanda was the daughter Wayne had with the girl he dated back in North Carolina, the girl that told me he didn't really love me and was only with me for JV. She and Wayne stayed together for a few short years and then broke it off. He ended up marrying Bailey, his close friend from high school.

It was difficult sleeping the night before the wedding knowing that my first daughter was about to be a married women. She spent the night at our house with her Matron of Honor and her fiancé Cyprian stayed at a hotel with his boys. The time spent with her was so special. It was also the same night of the Scandal season finale that, of course, we had no time to watch. I used to have Scandal parties for every opening and closing season. What a scandal it was that the final episode occurred on the night before my daughter's wedding. We spent the entire evening finishing the guest list seating, laughing with our family, enjoying all of the excitement of the time and counting down to the hour that JV would walk down the aisle to meet Cyprian. At the end of the day, it was a beautiful event and nothing could have made me more proud then the moment my first daughter married the love of her life. About a week before she'd asked me to join her with her Dad to walk her down the aisle, and it was my honor to do so.

When the year 2018 came to an end, Spencer and I decided to get a room at the Allegria hotel in order to wake up on the beach on New Year's Eve and take a break from the house and all the years' memories. While we sat in front of the window on the Long Beach boardwalk I was taking pictures of Spencer with my phone and just as he was about to take a picture of me, my phone rang. The contact information said "Daddy" and my heart dropped. On the other end of the line was my little brother Eric. He was calling to tell me my Dad had passed away.

Daddy

For the past nine years Daddy had not been well. I visited him every year in Florida and each year you could see his reduction in stature and in weight, but never in his spirit. He was slowly deteriorating with a host of ailments. Daddy had gone into the hospital the day after Christmas with pneumonia. This was his third time in the hospital since he had been sick. He had already been suffering with prostate cancer, dementia, had lost his vision about a year before, and he was bed ridden. He ended up with sepsis, an infection in his blood. Ultimately, he never recovered, and the sepsis took his life.

Daddy lived a long life, to the age of 89, and we sent him home honorably like the king he was. His hands had formed into an ataxia after many years of little movement. He had his hands pursed in the form of fists like a fighter while lying in his coffin before heading to his final resting place in Hudson, Florida outside of Spring Hill where he lived. Daddy was my fighter, my supporter and my hero. He will forever live in the grave in my soul as a positive memory, because he changed my life. We had many moments of close times and our share of distance. When I had JV he assumed that having a baby would naturally interfere with my education. Education was a major requirement of acceptance, success and favor in my father's eyes. Ultimately, my father did the best he could to provide for us after coming here from Jamaica and making a life for us. He taught me the importance of good credit, taking care of your home, your driveway, your lawn, and the importance of hard work, consistency, building good relationships, going to church and having faith in God. I will never forget how much he loved Chinese food, his lazy boy chair, Wray & Nephew white rum and the races at Belmont Racetrack. I brought his clothes for him that he wore in his coffin, including a tie that had race horses on them. It was the least I could do to take care of him before he went off to his final resting place. More importantly, I will never forget his love for me and the special bond we shared.

It was difficult losing my father at a time when it was so important to have him in my life. Now, in September 2019, the day of what would have been my father's 90th birthday is coming up, and it's been 10 years since I started writing this book. Throughout it all, I still remain his little girl. I am a Vice President in a healthcare company. I am a PhD candidate for a doctorate in Business and

Human Resources. I have given myself one year to complete my dissertation. I find myself still trying to prove to him that I can complete my education to the highest degree based on his concern many years ago that having a child would set me back from my educational goals. I encourage his grandchildren and great grandchildren (who sadly he was never able to meet) to be the best they can be every day. I am still busy being his daughter in his absence. In the past I was always looking for love and approval from him and others, at times in all the wrong places.

The things both my parents taught me over time and the love we shared are the foundation I will build upon for the rest of my life from this point forward. I hope to use what I have learned in my lifetime to mentor others who want to get past the decisions they've made that harbor deep feelings of guilt, resentment and fear. Although I have come across many consequences in life that brought on many regrets, lessons and blessings, I wouldn't change them for the world since in essence they have made me the woman I am today; ambitious, loving and faithful. All of those negative emotions, although difficult to get past, can now be let go. I have sent them all to the Grave in My Soul…